POWER BLENDS AND SMOOTHIES

Catherine Atkinson

A How To Book

ROBINSON

ROBINSON

First published in Great Britain in 2015 by Robinson

Copyright © Catherine Atkinson, 2015

Important note
The material contained in this book is for general guidance and does not deal with particular circumstances, nor is it intended as a substitute for medical advice on a personal and individual basis. Any person with a condition requiring medical attention should consult a qualified medical practitioner.

A CIP catalogue record for this book
is available from the British Library.

ISBN: 978-1-47213-656-5 (paperback)
ISBN: 978-1-47213-657-2 (ebook)

Typeset by Basement Press, Glaisdale
Printed and bound in Great Britain by CPI Group (UK) Ltd,
Croydon CRO 4YY

Papers used by Robinson are from well-managed forests
and other sustainable sources

MIX
Paper from
responsible sources
FSC® C104740

Robinson
is an imprint of
Little, Brown Book Group
Carmelite House
50 Victoria Embankment
London EC4Y 0DZ

An Hachette UK Company
www.hachette.co.uk

www.littlebrown.co.uk

How To Books are published by Robinson, an imprint of Little, Brown Book Group. We welcome proposals from authors who have first-hand experience of their subjects. Please set out the aims of your book, its target market and its suggested contents in an email to Nikki.Read@howtobooks.co.uk.

Catherine Atkinson has a degree in Food and Nutrition and has worked in various restaurants, including the Roux Brothers' famous patisserie. She has been Deputy Cookery Editor on *Woman's Weekly* and later Cookery Editor of *Home*. Catherine is now a full-time writer and food consultant to various food and lifestyle magazines and has written more than fifty cookbooks, including *Cookies, Biscuits, Bars and Brownies* (winner in the best dessert category of the Gourmand World Awards). She is also the author of *How To Make Perfect Panini*, *How To Make Your Own Cordials and Syrups* and *Everyday Bread from Your Bread Machine*.

Also available from Robinson

The High Speed Blender Cookbook

Everyday Family Recipes for Your Combination
Microwave

Everyday Lebanese Cooking

A Lebanese Feast of Vegetables, Pulses, Herbs and Spices

Pâtisserie

How To Make Your Own Cordials and Syrups

Southern Italian Family Cooking

How To Make Perfect Panini

Traditional Country Preserving

Afternoon Tea

Everyday Thai Cooking

Everyday Curries

The Healthy Slow Cooker Cookbook

Everyday Bread from Your Bread Machine

CONTENTS

INTRODUCTION

If you feel tired and sluggish, if stress is taking its toll and making you feel older than your years, if you find your immune system is flagging and you are frequently picking up minor ailments, or if you are struggling to lose a few pounds or simply don't want to gain any more, fruit and vegetable blends, smoothies and shakes could make a huge improvement to your well-being. Not only will you feel better, but you will look better too, as many of the nutrients found in fruit and vegetables help the body to get rid of toxins, leading to a clearer complexion, healthier hair and stronger nails.

Packed with revitalising and rejuvenating ingredients, power blends fit into hectic lives and make it easy to ensure that you get the recommended daily five to seven portions of fruit and vegetables, containing all the antioxidants, vitamins and minerals you need. Blending releases these nutrients and allows your body to utilise them easily, ensuring optimum nutrition. Smoothies made in a power blender are different from juices made in a juicer as they retain all the goodness and fibre of the fruit or vegetables used. Fibre is not only important for a healthy digestion, but helps to keep blood sugar levels stable and aids cardiovascular health.

Commercially made blends and smoothies are convenient but often contain added water, flavourings, preservatives and sweeteners and some are heat-treated to prolong their shelf life. Nothing beats the flavour and freshness of making your own, along with the reassurance of knowing exactly what it contains and being able to adjust the ingredients to your own personal taste.

You'll find 150 blends and smoothies in the following pages, conveniently divided into four chapters; health improvers, weight busters, exercise enhancers and beauty boosters. Whether you are looking for a low-calorie meal replacement to help with weight loss, a blend to replace fluid and electrolytes after exercise, or just a refreshing, delicious and nutritious shake, you will discover it here. Make blends and smoothies part of your daily routine; they couldn't be easier to prepare, or more enjoyable to drink.

TEN TOP TIPS FOR POWER BLENDS AND SMOOTHIES

- Most blends and smoothies here make a single serving, but some make enough to serve two, which is indicated in the recipe. Most power blenders come with a single-serving blender cup and a larger one, which can be used when you want to double up quantities.
- Use organic fruit and vegetables where possible. Wash fresh produce before blending and peel non-organic vegetables, such as carrots. Choose and use fresh fruit and vegetables at their peak when fully ripe. Store carefully and don't be tempted to blend over-ripe or bruised fruit; it will spoil the smoothie and lack nutrients.
- When preparing smoothies with bulky ingredients, such as melon and fresh greens, it can be difficult to fit them all in. Roughly chop before adding ingredients to the blender cup, and when you reach the maximum level blend briefly to reduce the volume, then add the remaining ingredients and blend again.
- Some of the more potent vegetable blends containing spirulina, chlorella or wheatgrass can take a bit of getting used to. The first time you make smoothies with these ingredients, add a little less than the recipe suggests and sip slowly. Gradually build up the

amount each time you make the smoothie. Always check the information on packets for the optimal and maximum 'dosage', as it may differ slightly between brands; this is usually around 10–15ml (2–3 tsp) a day.

- Many power blenders cope well with ice cubes; others do not, and adding ice may blunt the blades. Check the manufacturer's instructions and if yours will grind ice, you can use this instead of some or all of the water or other liquid. To get your measurements right, put the ice in a measuring jug and pour over the liquid you are using until it reaches the volume stated in the recipe.

- Some fruits and vegetables produce very thick blends and you may prefer to dilute them by adding a little more milk or complementary fruit juice. If the blend is well flavoured, dilute with a little water or add a few ice cubes to the glass.

- If, after blending, you feel your smoothie is too thin, add a complementary fruit or vegetable to thicken the mixture; good thickening choices include bananas and avocados. Alternatively, try 5–10ml (1–2 tsp) of lecithin granules (see page 9) or a large spoonful of Greek yogurt.

- Everyone's tastes differ and if you feel your blend is a little bland, a dash of lime or lemon juice can really bring out the flavour, especially with tropical and berry fruits. You can also add salt (if you are not on a low-salt diet) and pepper to savoury vegetable blends, or a pinch of dried red chillies or your favourite herbs or spices.

- Some ingredients, such as pineapple and fresh coconut, make very fibrous smoothies; if preferred, pour your finished smoothie through a fine or medium sieve, which will allow some of the smaller fibres to go through, but remove larger ones. To extract a little more juice, return the fibres in the sieve to the blender with a tiny amount of water and blend then sieve again.

- Some of the recipes here contain freshly grated ginger. Rather than preparing a piece of fresh ginger each time, peel, then finely grate a large piece of fresh ginger and freeze in ice cube trays, filling some to the top and half filling others. When frozen, turn out and store in a small freezer bag. Half-cubes will be the equivalent of 2.5ml (½ tsp), filled ones, 5ml (1 tsp). The cubes can be added to the blender while still frozen and will help to cool the blend.

SUPERFOODS

Also known as 'super-nutrients', these are nutrient-dense, calorie-sparse sources of antioxidants and essential nutrients that we need, but cannot make ourselves. Many are easy to add to smoothies and blends in fresh, dried or powdered form and have benefits including strengthening immunity and fighting free-radicals, which can damage cells. Fresh superfoods, such as green leafy vegetables and all kinds of fruit, are included in the recipes, but there are also a number of dried and powdered superfoods, which can improve the nutritional content of your blends. Before adding, check the dosage recommended on the pack, as strengths may vary from one brand to another.

GREEN SUPERFOODS

Wheatgrass
The sprouted grass of a wheat seed, wheatgrass contains high concentrations of chlorophyll, vitamins, minerals and all essential amino acids. It is highly regarded for detoxifying and also has anti-ageing, anti-inflammatory and cholesterol-reducing properties. Because it is a sprouted green and no longer a grain, it is suitable for those with wheat allergies.

Barleygrass

This has a milder flavour than wheatgrass, so is preferred by some. It is high in calcium, iron and vitamin C and is also a good source of vitamin B12, which may benefit those on a vegetarian diet. It has anti-viral and anti-inflammatory properties and, as a high-chlorophyll food, it destroys free-radicals in the body.

Spirulina

This dark blue-green micro-algae is particularly high in protein, iron and chlorophyll. It can help to control sugar levels, so may be helpful for diabetics, and can be used to treat liver damage and inhibit the growth of yeast, fungi and bacteria in the body.

Chlorella

A freshwater algae, this helps to detoxify and protect the immune system. It also encourages cell renewal and repair and is anti-inflammatory, so may relieve arthritis. Chlorella contains a higher amount of omega-3 and protein than both wheatgrass and spirulina.

Powdered greens

This is ideal if you want to buy just one type of green superfood; some brands contain as many as thirty different ingredients, but most blends are a mixture of wheatgrass, chlorella and spirulina, plus small amounts of other ingredients, such as probiotics and flaxseed.

FRUIT SUPERFOODS

Goji berries

These bright, orange-red, vine-grown berries from the Himalayas are a very rich source of vitamin C and also contain vitamins A, B1, B2, B6 and E. They are usually sold as dried berries or a powder and are often referred to as the 'longevity fruit' as they contain two amino acids that work together to boost skin renewal and repair.

Acai berries

Grown in the Amazon, these purple berries are similar in appearance to blueberries and are usually sold either as a concentrated juice, freeze-dried or as a powder. Acai berries can aid weight loss by reducing cravings and boosting metabolism. They have powerful anti-ageing and antioxidant properties due to a high level of anthocyanins. Acai berry powder adds a rich, deep-purple colour to smoothies, and a slight chocolatey flavour.

Baobab powder

Ground from the fruit of the baobab, which grows on one of the largest trees in Madagascar, this is packed with vitamin C and the B-group vitamins and is rich in many minerals including calcium, iron, potassium and zinc. It boosts energy levels and the immune system, and its citrus flavour, sometimes described as a combination of grapefruit, pear and vanilla, works well in both fruit- and vegetable-based blends.

Camu-camu

This purplish-red, berry-like fruit grows in South America and contains the highest levels of vitamin C of any fruit. Anti-viral and anti-inflammatory, it is naturally energising and mood-lifting. The flavour of camu-camu has a hint of caramel.

Lacuma

This sub-tropical fruit is high in antioxidants, calcium, iron and vitamins C and B3. It has a subtle caramel flavour and colour, and makes an excellent alternative to sugar as it is naturally very sweet.

NUT, SEED AND ROOT SUPERFOODS

Raw cacao

High in protein and packed with an abundance of magnesium, which helps to support electrolyte balance, raw cacao is also a good source of iron, zinc and theobromine, a mild, mood-lifting stimulant. Raw cacao differs from cocoa powder, as the temperature during processing does not exceed 40ºC, so heat-sensitive vitamins and anti-oxidants are retained. It has an intense, unsweetened chocolate flavour.

Coconut

Coconuts are among the highest sources of electrolytes in nature, which is why coconut water (the liquid inside young green coconuts) is often considered a good drink during and after exercise.

Chia seeds

These tiny black seeds are one of the richest plant sources of omega-3 fatty acids and are also a source of complete protein, containing all the essential amino acids. When added to liquid they absorb around ten times their weight in water, so they work well as a thickener in blends and may help with weight loss, keeping you feeling fuller for longer.

Flaxseed

Available as small golden or brown seeds or ground into a coarse powder. The latter is better for smoothies, as it blends much more successfully. A rich source of omega-3 fatty acids, flaxseed is also one of the best sources of lignans, a plant oestrogen that may reduce the risk of prostate, breast and colon cancers.

Maca

Ground from the maca root, which grows in South America, this has been cultivated for centuries in the belief that it can increase fertility and enhance libido. Maca helps to regulate hormone imbalances and is recommended during the menopause. It has a mild, malty flavour that goes well with milk and yogurt-based blends.

OTHER SUPERFOODS

Purple corn
Ground into a deep-purple powder, this is a good source of anthocyanin, which protects the heart and boosts your cancer defences. It has a subtle corn flavour, so is good in vegetable blends and strong-tasting fruit ones.

Milk thistle
Usually sold as a liquid, this is made from the black seeds harvested from the milk thistle flower and contains silymarin, which detoxifies the liver, helps to protect it from the damaging effects of alcohol and repairs damaged cells.

Lecithin granules
Lecithin is needed by every living cell in the human body and is a natural source of inositol and choline – two nutrients that play an important role in fat metabolism. It helps the body to break down and dispose of low-density lipoprotein (LDL) cholesterol. Some claim that it can help to promote weight loss, although this benefit is still controversial. The creamy-beige granules are derived from soya beans and act as a thickener and emulsifier, helping to prevent blends from separating.

SWEETENING BLENDS AND SMOOTHIES

The best way of ensuring smoothies and blends are sufficiently sweet is to choose ripe produce at its peak. Many non-dairy milks, such as rice and nut milks, also have a naturally sweet flavour (avoid sweetened varieties, where possible). If, in addition to the natural sweetness provided by ripe fruit and vegetables, you want to add sweeteners, avoid refined sugars and instead opt for honey, lacuma powder or maple syrup. Alternatively, add a little agave syrup, which is sweeter than refined sugar and has a lower glycaemic index.

MAKING NUT MILKS

While shop-bought cartons of nut milk are convenient, they often contain a higher proportion of sugar than nuts, as well as additional ingredients, such as flavourings, thickeners and preservatives. Homemade nut milks are healthy, fresh and additive-free. They allow you to have complete control of the ingredients included and the final taste and thickness of the milk. A wide range of nut 'milks' can be made simply by blending shelled, raw, unsalted nuts with water, including almonds, cashews and hazelnuts, which are all featured in this book.

ALMOND NUT MILK

This is probably the most popular commercially made nut milk and has a subtle, almost neutral flavour, which makes it ideal if you want to blend it with other flavourings. Because almonds are a relatively hard nut, they take a long time to soak (this is essential to soften the nut so that it will blend smoothly), but if it is more convenient, you can leave them to soak overnight. This method of making nut milk can be applied to most nuts.

Makes 450ml (¾ pint)

75g (3oz) blanched almonds
450ml (¾ pint) filtered water, plus soaking water
pinch of sea salt (optional)

1   Put the almonds in a large glass, ceramic or stainless-steel bowl and pour over enough water to cover by about 2.5cm (1in). Filtered water is preferable, but tap water can be used for soaking. Add a small pinch of sea salt as well if you like; this will help soften the nuts, but isn't essential and should be left out if you are on a low-sodium diet. Leave the nuts to soak for 8–12 hours to soften and plump up as they absorb the soaking water. You can do this at room temperature for up to 8 hours, but put them in the fridge if you are soaking for any longer.

2   After soaking, tip the almonds into a large sieve or colander to drain. Briefly rinse the nuts, then drain again and tip into a powerful blender.

3 Add about a third of the filtered water. Pulse the blender a few times to break up the almonds, then blend continuously for about 1 minute. Add a further third of the water and blend for a further minute, until the mixture is well blended and smooth.

4 Even though almonds produce a smooth milk, straining will give it a silkier texture and remove any fine pieces of nuts that haven't completely blended. Pour the mixture through a very fine-meshed plastic or stainless-steel sieve into a large bowl. For a smoother result, line the sieve with muslin, or pour the mixture through a reusable nut bag placed over a jug. Leave it to filter at its own pace for a few minutes, then gently stir the pulp to encourage the liquid to pass through more quickly. To extract a little more nut milk from the pulp, slowly pour the remaining third of the filtered water over the nut pulp and leave to drain again.

5 When the milk has filtered through, gather up the corners of the muslin or nut bag and gently squeeze with clean hands to extract the last few drops of nut milk.

6 The milk is now ready to use in blends and smoothies. If you want to use it straight away, serve your blend over a few ice cubes to chill the drink. Otherwise, store the nut milk in the fridge (see next page), then use it chilled in your recipes.

OTHER NUT MILKS

Other nut milks can be made in exactly the same way, but have different soaking times. Soak Brazil nuts and cashews for 3–6 hours, hazelnuts, pecans and walnuts for 4–6 hours.

NUT MILK STORAGE AND SHELF LIFE

Homemade nut milk should be kept in the fridge in a glass jug with a lid or covered with cling film. Avoid plastic or metal, as these can taint the flavour of the milk. It will stay fresh for up to three days. After a day or two, the milk may separate, so always give it a stir or shake before using.

THICKENING AND EMULSIFYING NUT MILKS

It is perfectly normal for nut milks to separate slightly after a day or two; you simply need to stir or shake before using. Alternatively you can add a natural emulsifier to the milk such as lecithin (see page 9). Blend up to 15ml (1 tbsp) of lecithin into every 450ml (¾ pint) nut milk after it has been strained.

1
HEALTH IMPROVERS

BREAKFAST BLEND

A great way to start the day, this smoothie is ideal for breakfast time as it is quick and nourishing, containing a good balance of protein, antioxidant vitamins, and minerals such as calcium, potassium and iron.

Serves 1

1 small ripe banana
small handful of kale, about 15g (½oz)
50g (2oz) fresh or frozen blueberries
5ml (1 tsp) wheat germ
45ml (3 tbsp) plain bio yogurt
200ml (7fl oz) chilled skimmed milk

1   Peel and slice the banana. Wash the kale and shake dry, removing any large, tough stems. Put the banana and kale in the blender with the blueberries, wheat germ, yogurt and milk.
2   Pulse the blender for a few seconds until the fruit and kale are finely chopped, then blend for about 30 seconds until smooth. Check the consistency; add a little more milk if you prefer a thinner smoothie and briefly blend again.

MANGO AND ORANGE WAKE-UP

This invigorating drink should ideally be made with fresh orange juice. It tastes better than shop-bought juice and is better for you, too, as even cartons of 'freshly squeezed' juice gradually lose their vitamin C content once opened.

Serves 2

1 medium ripe mango
1 medium carrot
1 small ripe banana
1 large orange
75ml (3fl oz) chilled filtered water
10ml (2 tsp) camu-camu powder (optional)
ice cubes, to serve

1   Cut a lengthwise slice on either side of the mango stone, then peel away the skin and chop the flesh from around the stone.
2   Peel and roughly chop the carrot and banana. Halve the orange and squeeze out the juice. Put the mango, carrot, banana and orange juice in the blender. Add the water and camu-camu powder, if using.
3   Pulse the blender for a few seconds until the fruit is finely chopped, then blend for about 45 seconds, until the mixture is smooth. Pour over ice cubes into two glasses.

COOK'S TIP
If preferred, halve the quantity of ingredients to make a smoothie for one.

EASY GREEN SMOOTHIE

This blend is perfect for those who haven't had a 'green smoothie' before and are a little reluctant to try. Despite containing a generous helping of nutritious kale, you'll taste only a hint of it in the creamy fruity flavour.

Serves 1

1 small ripe banana
75g (3oz) fresh or frozen strawberries
small handful kale, about 15g (½oz)
150ml (¼ pint) chilled coconut water or filtered water
2.5ml (½ tsp) pure vanilla extract

1   Peel and slice the banana. Wash, hull and halve the strawberries if using fresh. Wash the kale and shake off excess water, then remove any large, tough stems.

2   Put the kale in the blender with the banana and strawberries, about two-thirds of the coconut or filtered water and the vanilla extract.

3   Pulse the blender for a few seconds until the fruit and kale are finely chopped, then blend for about 30 seconds until smooth. Check the consistency and add a little more coconut water or water if you prefer a thinner smoothie and briefly blend again.

COOK'S TIP
If you prefer, use 150g (5oz) bought frozen strawberry and banana smoothie mix instead of the fresh fruit (making sure you have a roughly equal amount of strawberries and banana slices).

GREEN CLEAN SWEEP

An ideal start to the week or for 'the morning after the night before', this is a great detoxifying drink. Lemon juice sharpens the flavour and also stops the other ingredients oxidising, helping to retain both the colour and nutrients.

Serves 1

1 ripe pear
½ celery stick
5cm (2in) piece cucumber
small handful of baby spinach leaves, about 15g (½oz)
freshly squeezed juice of half a small lemon
5ml (1 tsp) chlorella powder (optional)
100ml (4fl oz) chilled filtered water

1 Wash the pear and vegetables and pat dry with kitchen paper. Quarter and core the pear then roughly chop the pear, celery and cucumber.

2 Put the pear and vegetables in the blender and add the lemon juice, chlorella power, if using, and chilled water.

3 Pulse the blender for a few seconds until the pear and vegetables are finely chopped, then blend for about 30 seconds until smooth. Check the consistency and add a little more water if you prefer a thinner smoothie and briefly blend again.

PAPAYA, PINEAPPLE AND GINGER DIGESTIVE

Both papaya (pawpaw) and pineapple contain enzymes that help to break down protein and aid digestion. Ginger adds a distinctive flavour and warmth to this drink and has many healing properties, especially as a remedy for sickness and nausea.

Serves 1

½ small papaya, about 175g (6oz)
¼ small fresh pineapple or half a 200g (7oz) can pineapple pieces in natural juice
2 Brazil nuts
2.5ml (½ tsp) grated fresh ginger (see page 3)
5ml (1 tsp) lime juice
175ml (6fl oz) chilled pineapple juice or filtered water or a mixture of both

1 Peel the papaya and scoop out and discard the seeds, then roughly chop the flesh. If using fresh pineapple, remove the skin and the central core if it is hard and roughly chop the flesh. If using canned pineapple, drain and reserve the juice.
2 Put the papaya, pineapple, Brazil nuts, ginger and lime juice in the blender. If using canned pineapple, make up the reserved juice to 175ml (6fl oz) with chilled water. Add the liquid to the blender.
3 Pulse the blender for a few seconds until the fruit is finely chopped, then blend for about 45 seconds until smooth.

SUPER DETOX

Strawberries contain ellagic acid, which helps the liver to remove toxins from the body. Combined with pink grapefruit, spinach and ginger, all effective detoxifiers, this is a super-cleansing drink.

Serves 1

100g (4oz) fresh or frozen strawberries
small handful of baby spinach leaves, about 15g (½oz)
1 pink grapefruit
2.5ml (½ tsp) grated fresh ginger (see page 3)
100ml (4fl oz) filtered water, chilled if using fresh fruit
5ml (1 tsp) acai berry powder (optional)

1   Wash and hull the strawberries if using fresh and cut in half if large. Wash the spinach and shake dry. Halve the pink grapefruit and squeeze out the juice.
2   Put the strawberries, spinach and grapefruit juice in the blender. Add the ginger and water, and the acai berry powder, if using.
3   Pulse the blender for a few seconds or until the strawberries and spinach are finely chopped, then blend for about 30 seconds until smooth.

PURPLE POWER

As well as helping to lower blood pressure, beetroot can increase the level of antioxidant enzymes in the body and boost the number of white blood cells, which are responsible for eliminating abnormal cells. This is a textured blend, so if you prefer a very smooth drink, pour it through a fine sieve before serving.

Serves 1

1 small, raw beetroot, about 150g (5oz)
50g (2oz) fresh or frozen blackberries
50g (2oz) red or black grapes
200ml (7fl oz) chilled water
3 drops milk thistle extract (optional)

1   Top and tail the beetroot, then thinly peel and cut into small chunks. If the beetroot has green leafy tops, trim and wash these and add to the blender with the beetroot.

2   Wash the blackberries if using fresh and the grapes and add to the blender with the water and milk thistle extract, if using.

3   Pulse the blender for a few seconds until the beetroot and fruit is finely chopped, then blend for about 45 seconds or until the mixture is fairly smooth.

IN THE PINK

This is great as a detox after over indulging; fresh pears, cucumber and ginger are blended with pink grapefruit juice to make a light and refreshing blend that's a cross between a juice and a smoothie.

Serves 1

1 ripe pear
handful of white grapes, about 50g (2oz)
¼ cucumber
1 pink grapefruit
2.5ml (½ tsp) grated fresh ginger (see page 3)
ice cubes, to serve

1 Wash the pear and grapes, then cut the pear into quarters and remove the core. Roughly chop into chunks with the cucumber.

2 Halve the pink grapefruit and squeeze out the juice. Put the pear, grapes, cucumber and grapefruit juice in a blender with the ginger.

3 Pulse the blender for a few seconds until the fruit and cucumber are finely chopped, then blend for about 45 seconds or until the mixture is smooth. Pour into a glass and add an ice cube or two to chill the drink.

BLUEBERRY BRAIN BOOSTER

Antioxidants in blueberries stimulate the flow of blood and oxygen to the brain and can help to boost concentration and memory for up to five hours after consumption. Drink this at breakfast or lunchtime and it should help keep you from flagging in the afternoon.

Serves 1

100g (4oz) fresh or frozen blueberries
pinch of ground cinnamon
2 Brazil nuts
250ml (8fl oz) chilled coconut drinking milk
5ml (1 tsp) goji berry powder (optional)

1   Wash the blueberries if using fresh, then put in a blender with the cinnamon, Brazil nuts and coconut drinking milk. Add the goji berry powder if using.
2   Pulse the blender for a few seconds until the blueberries and nuts are finely chopped, then blend for about 45 seconds, or until the mixture is very smooth.

RASPBERRY MUESLI SMOOTHIE

This is perfect when you don't have time to sit down and eat a 'proper' breakfast in the morning. Use a good-quality muesli; one with added dried fruits, such as apricots and dates, will work well and will thicken the smoothie and add a creamy texture.

Serves 1

100g (4oz) fresh or frozen raspberries
a handful of muesli, about 25g (1oz)
200ml (7fl oz) chilled semi-skimmed or skimmed milk
30ml (2 tbsp) plain bio yogurt

1 Put the fresh or frozen raspberries in a blender, then add the muesli, milk and yogurt.
2 Pulse the blender for a few seconds or until the ingredients are finely chopped, then blend for about a minute, or until the mixture is smooth. Check the consistency (the thickness will depend on the muesli you have used) and add a little more milk if liked, then briefly blend again.

COOK'S TIP
If you remember, soak the muesli and milk in the fridge overnight; it will plump up and soften the fruit and oats and the smoothie will be thicker and smoother.

PEAR AND KIWI FEEL-GOOD

This green smoothie is enhanced with ginseng, which can help to reduce tiredness, alleviate stress and boost the immune system. It is often bought in tablet form, but is also available as a powder, which is ideal for adding to smoothies.

Serves 1

1 ripe pear
handful of seedless white grapes, about 50g (2oz)
1 ripe kiwi fruit
5ml (1 tsp) ginseng powder
175ml (6fl oz) chilled unsweetened apple juice or a mixture
   of juice and filtered water

1 Wash the pear and grapes. Quarter and core the pear and cut into chunks. Thinly peel the skin from the kiwi and roughly cut into chunks or slices. Put the pear, grapes and kiwi into a blender.
2 Sprinkle the ginseng powder over the fruit and pour over the apple juice.
3 Pulse the blender for a few seconds until the fruit is finely chopped, then blend for about 45 seconds or until the mixture is smooth.

TOMATO AND GARLIC PEP-ME-UP

Although eating raw garlic is a little anti-social, it has great antiviral, antibacterial and antifungal properties. Tomatoes are a good source of vitamins C and E and contain the bioflavonoid lycopene, which can reduce the effects of free-radicals.

Serves 1

1 carrot
2 vine-ripened tomatoes
¼ red pepper
1 small garlic clove, peeled
5ml (1 tsp) ground flaxseed
pinch ground turmeric
5ml (1 tsp) barleygrass powder (optional)
100ml (4fl oz) chilled filtered water
small pinch of salt (optional)
freshly ground black pepper

1 Peel and roughly chop the carrot. Wash and quarter the tomatoes, and remove the seeds from the red pepper and slice. Put all the vegetables in a blender with the garlic, flaxseed and turmeric.
2 Add the barleygrass powder, if using, and pour in the water. If liked, season with salt and pepper.
3 Pulse the blender for a few seconds until the vegetables are finely chopped, then blend for about a minute or until the mixture is smooth.

MINTY AVOCADO AND PEAR

Although avocados have a high fat content, it is mono-unsaturated fat, so it can help to lower blood cholesterol levels. They also contain valuable amounts of vitamins C and E, and iron, potassium and manganese. Fresh mint can help to calm the digestive tract and adds a subtle aromatic touch.

Serves 2

1 small or medium ripe avocado
10ml (2 tsp) lime juice
1 ripe pear
175ml (6fl oz) chilled filtered water
leaves from 2 sprigs of mint

1 Cut the avocado in half and remove the stone. Scoop out the flesh and put in the blender, then sprinkle over the lime juice.
2 Wash the pear, cut it into quarters and remove the core. Roughly chop and add to the blender with the water and mint leaves.
3 Pulse the blender for a few seconds until the avocado and pear are finely chopped, then blend for about 45 seconds or until the mixture is smooth. Divide between two glasses.

RASPBERRY RESTORER

Raspberries are rich in energy and brain-boosting B-vitamins. Here, their sweet and slightly tart flavour is combined with soothing and nutritious rice milk and chia seeds, the richest plant source of omega-3.

Serves 1

15ml (1 tbsp) chia seeds
250ml (8fl oz) chilled rice milk
100g (4oz) fresh or frozen raspberries
2.5ml (½ tsp) pure vanilla extract or rose water

1 Put the chia seeds in a bowl or a blender, pour over the rice milk and leave to soak in the fridge for at least 30 minutes, or overnight if preferred (the chia seeds will swell and soften).

2 If soaked in a bowl, tip the chia mixture into a blender. Add the raspberries and vanilla or rose water.

3 Pulse the blender for a few seconds, then blend for about 30 seconds, or until the mixture is smooth and creamy.

APRICOT AND ALMOND FLUSH

Dried fruit is useful when the fruit bowl is empty, although it is best pre-soaked when making smoothies. High in fibre and packed with iron, dried apricots are good blended with a juice rich in vitamin C to help absorb this mineral. A few almonds add creaminess and protein to the blend.

Serves 1

50g (2oz) dried apricots
50g (2oz) blanched almonds
100ml (4fl oz) filtered water
100ml (4fl oz) chilled unsweetened apple juice
30ml (2 tbsp) plain bio yogurt

1 Put the apricots and almonds in a bowl and pour over the filtered water. Cover the bowl with cling film and leave to soak for at least 3 hours, or overnight in the fridge.
2 Tip the apricots, nuts and soaking water into a blender. Add the apple juice and yogurt, pulse for a few seconds or until finely chopped, then blend for about 45 seconds until smooth.

COOK'S TIP
Choose dark-coloured dried apricots if you can find them, rather than the bright orange ones, as they won't have been treated with the preservative sulphur.

CREAMY COCONUT COOLER

Coconuts have antibacterial, antiviral and antifungal properties that can help to destroy harmful bacteria, viruses and fungal infections and can also boost your immune system. This is one of the few blends that should be strained to make a smoother drink.

Serves 1

40g (1½oz) blanched hazelnuts
100g (4oz) chopped coconut flesh from a fresh coconut
300ml (½ pint) coconut water
few drops pure vanilla extract (optional)
ice cubes, to serve

1   Put the hazelnuts in a bowl and pour over enough filtered water to cover by at least 2.5cm (1in). Cover and leave to soak for at least 3 hours, or overnight in the fridge.
2   Drain the hazelnuts and put in a blender with the coconut, coconut water and vanilla, if using. Pulse the blender for a few seconds or until the hazelnuts and coconut are finely chopped, then blend for 1 minute or until the mixture is fairly smooth.
3   Pour the mixture into a muslin-lined sieve or a nut bag over a wide jug and leave to drain (you may need to do this in two batches). When the nut milk has finished draining, gather up the corners of the muslin or gently twist the nut bag to squeeze out the last few drops. If liked, you can return the pulp to the blender with 75ml (3fl oz) filtered water and repeat the blending and straining process to extract a little more nut milk. Discard the pulp and serve the milk with an ice cube or two.

COOK'S TIP
You can often buy chunks of ready-prepared fresh coconut in supermarkets; look for it in the ready-prepared fresh fruit section of the chiller cabinets.

ROCKET FUEL

Fresh rocket has a lovely peppery flavour and contains a range of beneficial vitamins and minerals, particularly iron, folate and the antioxidants vitamin C and beta-carotene. Here, the rocket is blended with tomatoes and mild-tasting cucumber to balance the flavour, and a pinch of red chilli to add a spicy kick.

Serves 1

small handful fresh rocket leaves, about 15g (½oz)
2 vine-ripened tomatoes
¼ cucumber
150ml (¼ pint) chilled filtered water
tiny pinch dried red chilli flakes
freshly ground black pepper

1 Wash the rocket leaves and shake off the excess water. Wash the tomatoes and cut into quarters. Roughly chop the cucumber.
2 Put all the ingredients into a blender. Pulse the blender for a few seconds until the vegetables are finely chopped, then blend for about 45 seconds, until the mixture is smooth.

MIXED VEGETABLE COCKTAIL

This blend of vegetables provides valuable vitamins and antioxidants. It also includes an optional addition of chlorella powder, which helps cells to renew and repair as well as containing protein and beneficial fatty acids, such as omega-3.

Serves 1

½ red pepper
¼ cucumber
¼ bulb fennel
small handful of kale, about 15g (½oz)
5ml (1 tsp) chlorella or powdered greens (optional)
150ml (¼ pint) chilled filtered water

1 Wash all the vegetables and shake the excess water from the kale, removing any large stems. Remove the seeds and white membranes from the red pepper, then roughly chop the pepper, cucumber and fennel. Put in a blender with the kale, add the chlorella or powdered greens, if using, then pour over the water.

2 Pulse the blender for a few seconds until the vegetables are finely chopped, then blend for about 1 minute, until the mixture is smooth.

MALTED STRAWBERRY AND CACAO SHAKE

Theobromine, found in raw cacao, is a mild, non-addictive stimulant that can lift the mood and may help with depression. Rather than sweetening this shake with sugar, malt extract is added, which is a natural sweetener and adds a delicious flavour.

Serves 1

100g (4oz) fresh or frozen strawberries
15ml (1 tbsp) raw cacao
10ml (2 tsp) barley malt extract
250ml (8fl oz) chilled semi-skimmed or skimmed milk
10ml (2 tsp) dried skimmed milk powder
ice cubes, to serve

1 Wash and hull the strawberries if using fresh. Put in a blender with the cacao, malt extract, milk and skimmed milk powder.
2 Pulse the blender for a few seconds until the strawberries are finely chopped, then blend for about 30 seconds, until smooth. Pour into a glass with a couple of ice cubes to chill the drink.

CRANBERRY, APPLE AND ORANGE CRUSH

As well as their anti-inflammatory properties, cranberries are effective in the treatment of cystitis and other urinary tract infections, as they can reduce levels of bacteria. They do have quite a tart flavour, so this blend has added sweetener.

Serves 1

1 eating apple
100g (4oz) fresh or frozen cranberries
10ml (2 tsp) agave syrup, maple syrup or honey
150ml (¼ pint) chilled orange juice or a mixture of orange
  juice and filtered water

1 Wash the apple, quarter, and remove the core. Cut each quarter in half and put in a blender with the cranberries, agave syrup, maple syrup or honey, and orange juice.
2 Pulse the blender for a few seconds or until the fruit is finely chopped, then blend for about 45 seconds, until smooth.

MANGO AND BANANA SMOOTHIE

Bananas often feature in both homemade and commercial smoothies because they add a creamy texture and thickness to the blend. Together with sesame seeds, they provide slow-release carbohydrate, which will help to perk you up if you are feeling a bit 'under the weather'.

Serves 1

1 small or medium ripe banana
½ ripe mango
5ml (1 tsp) honey
15ml (1 tbsp) sesame seeds
pinch of freshly grated nutmeg
1 large orange
30–60ml (2–4 tbsp) cold water

1   Peel the banana and slice or break into smaller pieces. Using a small, sharp knife, skin half the mango, then slice the flesh off the stone. Put the banana and mango in a blender with the honey, sesame seeds and nutmeg.

2   Cut the orange in half and squeeze out the juice. Add to the blender with 30ml (2 tbsp) of the water.

3   Pulse the blender for a few seconds until the fruit is finely chopped, then blend for about 45 seconds, until very smooth. Check the consistency and if you prefer your drink a little thinner, add the remaining 30ml (2 tbsp) of water and blend again.

COLD COMFORT

Here banana is blended with milk and flavoured with a comforting trio of ginger, cinnamon and honey. It won't cure a cold, but will cool and soothe a sore throat and is a great pick-me-up when you don't feel like eating. Camu-camu adds a hint of caramel and boosts the immune system.

Serves 1

1 medium ripe banana
5ml (1 tsp) grated fresh ginger (see page 3)
2.5ml (½ tsp) ground cinnamon
10ml (2 tsp) honey
10ml (2 tsp) camu-camu powder (optional)
250ml (8fl oz) chilled semi-skimmed or skimmed milk
ice cubes, to serve

1   Peel and slice the banana or break into smaller pieces. Put in the blender with the ginger, cinnamon, honey and camu-camu powder, if using. Pour in the milk.
2   Blend for 30–45 seconds or until smooth. Pour into a glass, adding a couple of ice cubes to keep the drink well chilled.

CHERRY AID

A natural anti-inflammatory, cherries are often recommended for those who suffer with arthritis and gout. Here they are blended with oat milk, a little kale and lacuma for sweetness.

Serves 1

150g (5oz) fresh or frozen pitted dark cherries
small handful of kale, about 15g (½oz)
2.5ml (½ tsp) pure vanilla extract (optional)
10ml (2 tsp) lacuma powder (optional)
250ml (8fl oz) chilled oat milk

1 Wash the cherries if using fresh, then wash the kale, shake off excess water and remove any large, tough stalks. Put the cherries and kale in a blender. Add the vanilla and lacuma powder, if using, then pour in the milk.
2 Pulse the blender for a few seconds or until the cherries and kale are finely chopped, then blend for 30–45 seconds until smooth.

CHERRY LEMON SIP

As well as having anti-inflammatory properties, cherries are packed with vitamin C and contain melatonin, which aids sleep, making this an ideal drink for colds and flu, when you need to rest in bed.

Serves 1

150g (5oz) fresh or frozen pitted dark cherries
175ml (6fl oz) orange juice or a mixture of orange juice and filtered water, chilled if using fresh fruit
10ml (2 tsp) freshly squeezed lemon juice
10ml (2 tsp) honey

1 Wash the cherries if using fresh and put in a blender with the orange juice, lemon juice and honey.
2 Pulse the blender for a few seconds until the cherries are finely chopped, then blend for 30–45 seconds until smooth.

BRAZIL AND BANANA BREEZE

Of all nuts, Brazils are the richest in selenium, which is a natural mood enhancer; just a single nut each day will ensure that you are never deficient in this vital mineral. Low in calories and containing no cholesterol, soya milk can also reduce the risk of certain cancers and heart disease.

Serves 1

1 small or medium ripe banana
1 large Brazil nut
10ml (2 tsp) lacuma powder (optional)
250ml (8fl oz) chilled unsweetened soya milk

1   Peel the banana and slice or break into smaller pieces. Put in a blender with the Brazil nut and lacuma powder if using. Pour over the soya milk.
2   Pulse the blender for a few seconds until the banana and Brazil nut are finely chopped, then blend for about 45 seconds or until very smooth.

FROZEN BERRY AND BANANA BLEND

Bags of berries mixed with banana slices are found in most supermarket freezer cabinets and are a useful standby. You can also freeze your own banana slices when you have too many bananas that have all ripened at the same time.

Serves 1

100g (4oz) frozen berries, such as strawberries, raspberries and currants
50g (2oz) frozen banana slices
250ml (8fl oz) semi-skimmed or skimmed milk

1 Put the frozen berries and banana slices in a blender. Pour over the milk.
2 Pulse the blender for a few seconds until the fruit is chopped, then blend for about 45 seconds until smooth.

COOK'S TIP
To freeze bananas, peel and thickly slice. Place in a single layer on a sheet lined with baking parchment and open-freeze for several hours until solid. Transfer the frozen slices to lidded freezer containers or a freezer bag and use within 4 weeks.

MERRY BERRY RIPPLE

This is another recipe that is easily made with ready-prepared frozen fruit. 'Summer fruits' are usually a mixture of raspberries, redcurrants, blackcurrants and blackberries. This combination can be a little tart, so here it is sweetened a little and rippled with smooth creamy Greek-style yogurt.

Serves 1

150g (5oz) frozen mixed summer fruits, preferably partially thawed
10ml (2 tsp) lacuma powder or agave syrup or honey
150ml (¼ pint) cranberry or apple juice
30ml (2 tbsp) Greek yogurt

1 Put the frozen berries in a blender. Add the lacuma powder, agave syrup or honey and pour over the fruit juice.
2 Pulse the blender for a few seconds until the fruit is finely chopped, then blend for about 30 seconds until smooth.
3 Pour half of the smoothie into a glass and spoon in 15ml (1 tbsp) of the yogurt, then pour in the rest of the smoothie and top with the remaining yogurt. Briefly stir with a long spoon to make a rippled effect.

COOK'S TIP
Buy Greek yogurt rather than 'Greek-style' yogurt if you can. Real Greek yogurt is thickened by straining plain yogurt, whereas 'Greek-style' often contains thickeners and other additives.

COFFEE AND CARDAMOM FRAPPE

Coffee is a stimulant and shouldn't be drunk in excess, but the occasional cupful can give you a much-needed boost during the day. Here it is given a Middle-Eastern flavour by blending with a little ground cardamom, which aids digestion, almond milk and a couple of dates to thicken and sweeten the blend.

Serves 1

5ml (1 tsp) good-quality instant coffee
15ml (1 tbsp) very hot (not boiling) water
2 ready-to-eat dates, such as Medjool
1.5ml (¼ tsp) ground cardamom
250ml (8fl oz) chilled almond milk
ice cubes, to serve

1 Put the coffee in a blender and spoon over the hot water. Swirl the blender until the coffee has completely dissolved.
2 Halve the dates and remove the stones, then add to the blender with the cardamom. Pour in the almond milk.
3 Pulse the blender for a few seconds until the dates are finely chopped, then blend for 45 seconds until smooth and frothy. Put a couple of ice cubes in a glass and pour over the frappé.

HIGH-VITALITY CHOCOLATE AND ORANGE MILK-SHAKE

This satisfying meal-in-a-glass is made with a combination of milk and thick yogurt, blended with banana and orange juice and a spoonful of wheat germ for extra B and E vitamins. It's ideal when you're in a hurry and much more nutritious than a sandwich or a can of soup.

Serves 1

1 small ripe banana
150ml (¼ pint) Greek yogurt
150ml (¼ pint) chilled skimmed milk
100ml (4fl oz) orange juice, preferably freshly squeezed
5ml (1 tsp) wheatgerm
15ml (1 tbsp) cacao powder
5ml (1 tsp) lacuma powder (optional)

1 Peel the banana and slice or break into smaller pieces. Put in a blender with the yogurt, milk, orange juice, wheat germ, cacao and lacuma powder if using.
2 Pulse the blender for a few seconds until the banana is finely chopped, then blend for about 45 seconds or until very smooth.

HALE AND HEARTY

Oats and almonds are both renowned for lowering cholesterol and together with the potassium content of banana and kale, which helps to lower blood pressure, this a great, heart-healthy smoothie.

Serves 1

1 small or medium ripe banana
a small handful of kale, about 15g (½oz)
15ml (1 tbsp) rolled oats
6 blanched almonds
250ml (8fl oz) chilled skimmed or semi-skimmed milk

1   Peel the banana and thickly slice or break into smaller pieces. Wash the kale and shake off excess water, removing any large stems, then put in a blender with the oats, almonds and milk.
2   Pulse the blender for a few seconds until the banana, oats, almonds and kale are finely chopped, then blend for about 45 seconds, until smooth.

BLUEBERRY BUZZ

Blueberries can help your concentration and alertness throughout the day. Here they are blitzed with oat milk and chlorella, which has many health-giving properties including fighting fatigue. Lecithin helps to thicken and stabilise the smoothie.

Serves 1

100g (4oz) fresh or frozen blueberries
5ml (1 tsp) chlorella powder or powdered greens
5ml (1 tsp) lecithin granules (optional)
250ml (8fl oz) chilled oat milk

1 Put the blueberries, chlorella or powdered greens and lecithin granules, if using, in a blender and pour over the chilled oat milk.
2 If the blueberries are frozen, pulse the blender for a few seconds, then blend for 30–45 seconds or until smooth. If you're using fresh blueberries, the initial pulsing should not be necessary.

SWEET AND SAVOURY GREEN SMOOTHIE

This green smoothie is made from a combination of dark greens and milder lighter flavours for a slightly sweet blend. Packed with vitamin C and fibre, it makes a good choice for any time of the day.

Serves 1

1 ripe kiwi fruit
1 green eating apple
small handful, about 15g (½oz) baby spinach leaves
5cm (2in) piece of cucumber
150ml (¼ pint) chilled filtered water or coconut water

1 Peel the kiwi and cut into chunks. Wash, quarter and core the apple. Rinse the spinach under cold running water, then shake off excess water. Put everything into a blender with the cucumber and pour over the water or coconut water.
2 Pulse the blender for a few seconds or until the fruit and vegetables are finely chopped, then blend for 30–45 seconds, until smooth.

DOUBLE-GREEN, PEAR AND BANANA BLAST

This blend has a double helping of greens, so is not for the faint-hearted! Use a sweet, well-flavoured apple to balance the flavour and mild-tasting cashew nuts to add a creamy texture and thicken the blend.

Serves 1

small handful kale, about 15g (½oz)
small handful baby spinach leaves, about 15g (½oz)
1 ripe pear
1 small ripe banana
25g (1oz) cashew nuts
200ml (7fl oz) chilled filtered water

1 Rinse the kale and spinach leaves under cold running water and shake dry. Pack into a blender; you may need to tear the leaves into smaller pieces and push down to fit all the ingredients in.

2 Wash, quarter and core the pear. Peel the banana and slice or break into several pieces. Add the pear, banana and cashew nuts to the blender. Pour in the water.

3 Pulse the blender for a few seconds or until the fruit, vegetables and nuts are finely chopped, then blend for about 1 minute, until very smooth.

SPRING CLEAN

This is an excellent detoxifier as well as providing iron, which the vitamin C in the lime juice and pear helps the body to absorb. Wheatgrass powder intensifies the flavour, but you can leave it out if you prefer.

Serves 1

large handful of young spring green leaves, about 20g (¾oz)
½ bunch watercress
few sprigs of fresh parsley
5cm (2in) piece of cucumber
1 ripe green-skinned pear
5ml (1 tsp) wheatgrass (optional)
10ml (2 tsp) freshly squeezed lime juice
150ml (¼ pint) chilled filtered water

1 Wash the leaves, parsley, cucumber and pear. Shake dry or pat on kitchen paper. Remove any large thick stems from the spring greens, watercress and parsley and discard. Put the spring greens, watercress and parsley in a blender.

2 Roughly chop the cucumber and quarter and core the pear. Add to the blender, sprinkling over the wheatgrass powder if using. Add the lime juice and water.

3 Pulse the blender for a few seconds until the ingredients are finely chopped, then blend for 30–45 seconds until smooth. Check the consistency and add a little more water if you prefer it a little thinner.

FIG AND OAT BLEND

This is a great stress-reliever, as soya milk contains compounds that promote the production of serotonin, which enhances your mood and can also help to regulate sleeping patterns. As well as being a good source of iron, figs also contain a lot of fibre, so can be useful for treating constipation.

Serves 1

30ml (2 tbsp) rolled oats
60ml (4 tbsp) boiling water
5 ready-to-eat dried figs
250ml (8fl oz) chilled unsweetened soya milk
5ml (1 tsp) lacuma powder (optional)

1   Put the oats in a small heatproof bowl and pour over the boiling water. Leave to soak and cool for 10 minutes. Meanwhile, remove the woody stems from the figs and roughly chop. Put in a blender with enough of the milk to just cover (this will start softening them and give a smoother blend). Keep the rest of the milk chilled.

2   When the oats have soaked, add them to the blender and pour in the rest of the soya milk and the lacuma powder, if using.

3   Pulse the blender for a few seconds until the figs are finely chopped, then blend for 30–45 seconds until smooth.

STRAWBERRY AND ORANGE YOGURT SMOOTHIE

Here, fruit is blended with 'bio' yogurt or you can buy one labelled 'live' as it will contain beneficial bacteria. The balance of gut bacteria can easily be upset by medication, such as antibiotics, and stress, so this drink can help to maintain a healthy digestive tract.

Serves 1

100g (4oz) fresh or frozen strawberries
finely grated zest of ½ and juice of 1 whole orange
30ml (2 tbsp) filtered water
45ml (3 tbsp) plain bio yogurt
5ml (1 tsp) honey or agave syrup (optional)

1 Wash and hull the strawberries, if using fresh. Put them in a blender with the orange zest, juice, water, yogurt and honey or agave syrup, if using.
2 Pulse the blender for a few seconds until the strawberries are finely chopped, then blend for 30–45 seconds until smooth.

CHERRY TOFU SMOOTHIE

Tofu is an excellent source of protein as it contains all eight amino acids as well as iron and calcium and makes fantastically smooth, creamy blends. Soya protein (from which tofu is derived) can help to lower levels of 'bad' LDL cholesterol.

Serves 1

100g (4oz) fresh or frozen pitted dark cherries
75g (3oz) silken tofu
150ml (¼ pint) chilled unsweetened soya milk
150ml (¼ pot) cherry soya yogurt or plain natural soya
  yogurt
6 blanched almonds

1 Wash the cherries if using fresh and put them in a blender with the tofu, soya milk, yogurt and almonds.
2 Pulse the blender for a few seconds, until the cherries and almonds are finely chopped, then blend for about 45 seconds until smooth.

GUAVA AND PASSION FRUIT SMOOTHIE

Guava have tiny, hard, white pips, which even the most powerful blender won't grind, so it is better to purée and sieve the fruit for this smoothie.

Serves 1

400g (14oz) can guava halves in natural juice
1 ripe passion fruit
150ml (¼ pint) chilled coconut drinking milk
5ml (1 tsp) baobab powder (optional)
ice cubes, to serve

1   Tip the guava halves and their juice into a blender and blend for about 20 seconds until smooth. Pour into a fine sieve over a jug, letting the purée run through for a minute or two, then rub with the back of a spoon to extract the last of the purée. Discard the pips in the sieve. Rinse out the blender and pour the purée into it.

2   Cut the passion fruit in half and scoop the seeds out into the sieve. Rub the pulp and juice through the sieve into the blender.

3   Add the coconut drinking milk and baobab powder, if using. Blend for about 15 seconds until smooth. Pour into a glass, adding an ice cube or two to chill the drink.

COOK'S TIP
Passion fruit seeds can be a little bitter when blended in a smoothie, so it is better to press out the juice through a sieve first. Make sure the fruit is really ripe before using: the skins should be puckered and dimpled.

PEACH MELBA DELIGHT

Canned peaches are a good alternative to fresh, and reduce preparation time, but make sure you buy those in natural juices rather than sugary syrup. Peaches, including canned ones, contain plenty of vitamin C and this can help the body to absorb iron in other foods; in this case from dried apricots.

Serves 1

2 dried apricots
45ml (3 tbsp) chilled filtered water
200g (7oz) can peaches in natural juice
50g (2oz) fresh or frozen raspberries
150ml (¼ pint) chilled canned or carton low-fat custard

1 Cut the dried apricots into quarters using clean kitchen scissors. Put in a small bowl, spoon over the water, cover and leave to soak in the fridge for half an hour or overnight, if preferred.

2 Tip the apricots and water into a blender. Add the peaches and their juice, raspberries and custard.

3 Pulse the blender for a few seconds until the fruit is finely chopped, then blend for about 30 seconds until smooth.

BONE BUILDER SMOOTHIE

Leafy green vegetables, yogurt and sesame seeds (found in tahini) are all great vegetarian sources of calcium, which is vital for building, maintaining and repairing bones. Make sure you get some vitamin D from a few minutes sitting in the sun as well, to help your body absorb the calcium.

Serves 1

small handful of baby spinach leaves, about 15g (½oz)
small handful of kale, about 15g (½oz)
few sprigs of parsley
½ ripe avocado
10ml (2 tsp) tahini
100ml (4fl oz) chilled filtered water
150ml (¼ pint) bio or plain natural yogurt

1   Wash the spinach leaves, kale and parsley and shake off excess water, then remove any tough stems. Remove the skin from the avocado. Put the greens and avocado, tahini, water and yogurt in a blender.
2   Pulse the blender for a few seconds or until the greens are finely chopped, then blend for about 45 seconds, until smooth.

ACAI ANTIOXIDANT BLAST

Acai fruit is exceptionally high in antioxidants and is available as a purée, juice or powder. The powder is perfect for smoothies, as it acts as a thickener and adds an intense, slightly chocolatey flavour.

Serves 1

75g (3oz) fresh or frozen pitted cherries
1 small ripe banana
7.5ml (1½ tsp) acai berry powder
250ml (8fl oz) chilled unsweetened almond milk

1   If using fresh cherries, wash and then pit them (remove the stones). Peel the banana and slice or break into smaller pieces. Put the cherries, banana, acai powder and milk into a blender.
2   Pulse the blender for a few seconds or until the fruit is finely chopped, then blend for about 30 seconds until smooth.

FRUITY FROZEN YOGURT

Rather than using bought frozen yogurt, which is often full of artificial additives, here Greek yogurt is frozen for a few hours, or overnight if it's easier, then blended with vitamin-rich berries to make a smooth, slushy smoothie.

Serves 1

200ml (7fl oz) Greek yogurt
75g (3oz) fresh or frozen berries, such as strawberries,
  cherries, raspberries or blackcurrants
5ml (1 tsp) honey or agave syrup
2.5ml (½ tsp) pure vanilla extract

1 Put the yogurt in a freezer container and freeze for 3 hours or overnight if preferred.
2 Wash the berries, if using fresh, and pat dry on kitchen paper. Put the berries in a blender with the frozen yogurt, honey or agave syrup and vanilla.
3 Pulse the blender for a few seconds to break up the frozen yogurt, then blend for about 30 seconds, until smooth. Eat immediately with a spoon or wait 10 minutes and drink.

COCONUT, BANANA AND LEMONGRASS SMOOTHIE

Coconut milk is rich in calcium and magnesium and is a great partner to bananas, which have an antacid effect in the stomach and protect against acid linked to indigestion and heartburn. Lemongrass contains manganese, which is good for stress and adds a subtle unique flavour to this blend.

Serves 1

1 medium ripe banana
½ stalk lemongrass
250ml (8fl oz) chilled coconut milk

1 Peel the banana and slice or break into smaller pieces. Remove the tough outer leaves from the lemongrass and discard, then roughly chop the lemongrass.
2 Put the banana in a blender with the lemongrass and pour over the coconut milk.
3 Pulse the blender for a few seconds until the banana and lemongrass are finely chopped, then blend for 30–45 seconds until very smooth (check that the lemongrass has completely blended).

BRAZIL NUT MILK BLEND

Nut milks are an excellent alternative to dairy milk and are simple to make. Brazil nuts and wheat germ are both great sources of selenium, an antioxidant that is part of an enzyme that protects cells from the damaging effects of free-radicals that may lead to cardiovascular disease.

Serves 1

75g (3oz) Brazil nuts
250ml (8fl oz) chilled filtered water, plus extra for soaking
5ml (1 tsp) wheat germ

1 Put the Brazil nuts in a jug and pour over enough filtered water to cover by about 5cm (2in). Cover with cling film and leave to soak for at least 4 hours or overnight in the fridge.

2 Drain the nuts and put in a blender. Pour over the chilled filtered water and add the wheat germ.

3 Pulse the blender for a few seconds until the nuts are finely chopped, then blend for about 45 seconds until smooth.

PRUNE AND APRICOT SMOOTHIE

Of all mineral deficiencies, iron is the most common, with pre-menopausal women and vegetarians most at risk. Dried fruit is an excellent source and this simple smoothie is an easy way to top up your iron intake.

Serves 1

50g (2oz) dried stoned prunes
50g (2oz) dried apricots
250ml (8fl oz) filtered water
30ml (2 tbsp) plain bio yogurt

1   Put the prunes and apricots in a bowl, pour over the water, cover with cling film and leave to soak in the fridge for at least 3 hours or overnight if you prefer.
2   Tip the fruit and soaking liquid into a blender and add the yogurt.
3   Pulse the blender for a few seconds until the fruit is finely chopped, then blend for about 30 seconds until smooth. Check the consistency and add a few more spoonfuls of water if you prefer it thinner, briefly blending again.

FIVE-A-DAY

Although recent recommendations suggest you should eat seven servings of fruit and vegetables a day, five-a-day is a really good start and fewer than one in five adults currently manage this; make sure you are one of them!

Serves 1

1 small ripe banana
1 kiwi fruit
6 medium strawberries
small handful of kale or baby spinach leaves, about 15g
  (½oz)
150ml (¼ pint) orange or apple juice
60ml (4 tbsp) chilled filtered water

1   Peel the banana and slice or break into smaller pieces. Peel the kiwi and roughly chop. Wash the strawberries, hull and halve. Wash the kale or spinach and shake off the excess water, removing any large stems. Put all the prepared fruit and vegetables in a blender and pour over the fruit juice and water.

2   Pulse the blender for a few seconds until the fruit and vegetables are finely chopped, then blend for about 30 seconds until smooth.

CALCIUM-RICH FRUIT SMOOTHIE

Calcium is an essential nutrient for everyone, but especially for children and adolescents, many of whom don't meet the recommended daily intake of this mineral. A fruit smoothie is a healthy and appealing way of reaching the targets and decreases the risk of osteoporosis in later life.

Serves 1

1 orange
6 medium strawberries
150ml (¼ pint) chilled semi-skimmed milk
125g (4½ oz) pot plain or fruit-flavoured yogurt
10ml (2 tsp) honey
small scoop of dairy ice cream or frozen yogurt, to serve

1   Using a small, sharp knife, peel the orange, removing all the bitter white pith. Remove the segments by cutting between the membranes and discard any pips. Put the orange segments in a blender.
2   Wash and hull the strawberries. Add to the blender with the milk, yogurt and honey.
3   Pulse the blender for a few seconds until the fruit is finely chopped, then blend for about 30 seconds until smooth. Serve topped with a small scoop of ice cream or frozen yogurt.

RASPBERRY, OAT AND SEED SMOOTHIE

Seeds are highly nutritious and a good source of protein, vitamins and minerals. Some, such as linseeds, are also rich in omega-3 fatty acids – essential for regulating blood pressure and immune responses – so make sure you have a wide range in your diet.

Serves 1

30ml (2 tbsp) mixed seeds, such as sunflower, pumpkin, sesame and linseeds
250ml (8fl oz) chilled oat milk
75g (3oz) fresh or frozen raspberries

1   If time allows, put the seeds in a small bowl and pour over a few spoonfuls of the oat milk. Cover and leave to soak in the fridge for 2–3 hours; this will soften the seeds and make the blend smoother.
2   Tip the seeds into a blender and add the milk and raspberries.
3   Pulse the blender for a few seconds until the fruit and seeds are finely chopped, then blend for about 30 seconds until fairly smooth.

PISTACHIO AND ALMOND LASSI

In India, lassis come in many flavours, but spices and nuts are especially popular. All unsalted nuts can help to reduce cholesterol levels and cut the risk of type 2 diabetes and cardiovascular disease, but pistachios are particularly effective.

Serves 1

50g (2oz) shelled, unsalted pistachio nuts
25g (1oz) blanched almonds
150ml (¼ pint) chilled unfiltered water, plus extra for
  soaking
5ml (1 tsp) lacuma powder (optional)
5ml (1 tsp) lecithin granules (optional)
100g (4oz) plain bio yogurt
ice cubes or crushed ice, to serve

1 Put the pistachio nuts and almonds in a bowl and pour over enough cold filtered water to cover them by about 5cm (2in). Leave to soak at room temperature for 6 hours, or overnight in the fridge.
2 Drain the nuts and put them in a blender. Add the chilled water and lacuma powder and lecithin, if using. Pulse the blender for a few seconds, then blend for about 45 seconds until fairly smooth.
3 Add the yogurt and blend for a further 30 seconds. Pour into a glass and serve with ice.

GREAT EXPECTATIONS

During pregnancy, your needs for calcium, iron and the B-vitamin folate all increase. This smoothie is great for a mid-morning or afternoon snack and provides all three of these nutrients.

Serves 1

50g (2oz) dried apricots
1 orange
small handful of baby spinach leaves, about 15g (½oz), or
  5ml (1 tsp) powdered greens
15ml (1 tbsp) cacao powder
200ml (7fl oz) chilled skimmed or semi-skimmed milk
15ml (1 tbsp) skimmed milk powder

1 Snip the dried apricots into small pieces with kitchen scissors and put in a small bowl. Cut the orange in half and squeeze out the juice. Pour the juice over the apricots, cover with cling film and leave to soak in the fridge for an hour.

2 If using fresh spinach, wash well and put in a blender. If not, add the powdered greens, with the apricots and juice, cacao powder, milk and skimmed milk powder.

3 Pulse the blender for a few seconds until the apricots are finely chopped, then blend for about 45 seconds until smooth.

SUPER SOPORIFIC SMOOTHIE

Sleep allows the mind to rest and the body to repair itself, so it's important to make sure you are getting enough. Camomile and lettuce are both known for their calming effect and for aiding sleep, so this is a great blend to enjoy before bedtime.

Serves 1

1 camomile tea bag
100ml (4fl oz) boiling filtered water
100ml (4fl oz) chilled filtered water
50g (2oz) seedless white grapes
50g (2oz) soft lettuce
2–3 drops milk thistle (optional)

1 Make the tea using the camomile tea bag and boiling water and leave to steep for 5 minutes, then remove and discard the tea bag. Leave the tea to cool.
1 Meanwhile, wash the grapes and lettuce and put in a blender. Add the cold camomile tea and chilled water and milk thistle, if using.
1 Pulse the blender for a few seconds until the grapes and lettuce are finely chopped, then blend for 30 seconds until smooth.

COOK'S TIP
If you are in a hurry to cool the tea, make it in a measuring jug and instead of adding chilled filtered water in the second step, make the tea up to the 200ml (7fl oz) mark with ice cubes.

2
WEIGHT BUSTERS

BREAKFAST SHAKE

This high-protein 'meal-in-a-glass' contains tofu, which is low in fat and cholesterol and gives the drink an amazing smooth, creamy texture. Blended with antioxidant- and vitamin C-rich blueberries and orange juice, it makes a great start to the day.

Serves 1

75g (3oz) fresh or frozen blueberries
75g (3oz) firm silken tofu
15ml (1 tbsp) rolled oats
250ml (8fl oz) orange juice or a mixture of orange juice and filtered water, chilled if using fresh fruit
5ml (1 tsp) acai berry powder (optional)

1 Wash the blueberries if using fresh and put in a blender with the tofu, oats, orange juice and acai berry powder, if using.
2 Pulse the blender for a few seconds until the blueberries and oats are finely chopped, then blend for about 30 seconds, until smooth.

STRAWBERRIES AND CREAM SMOOTHIE

There isn't actually any cream in this smoothie, but almond milk and lecithin give it a lovely creamy taste and texture. This is a blend to sip slowly and enjoy as a healthy low-fat treat.

Serves 1

75g (3oz) fresh or frozen strawberries
1 small ripe banana
45ml (3 tbsp) low-fat bio yogurt
200ml (7fl oz) chilled unsweetened almond milk (choose a
   lower-calorie version)
5ml (1 tsp) lecithin granules
2.5ml (½ tsp) pure vanilla extract

1   Wash the strawberries if using fresh, hull them and halve if
    they are large. Peel the banana and slice or break into smaller
    pieces. Add the fruit to a blender with the yogurt, almond
    milk, lecithin and vanilla.
2   Pulse the blender for a few seconds until the strawberries are
    finely chopped, then blend for about 30 seconds, until
    smooth.

LYCHEE AND RASPBERRY BLEND

Lychees are very low in calories, yet just 3–4 raw or canned fruit will provide almost an entire day's requirement of vitamin C. Here they are blended with raspberries and rose water for a fragrant drink.

Serves 1

400g (14oz) can lychees in natural juice or light syrup
50g (2oz) fresh or frozen raspberries
45ml (3 tbsp) filtered water
2.5ml (½ tsp) rose water
ice cubes, to serve

1 Put the lychees and their juice or syrup into a blender. Add the raspberries, water and rose water.
2 Blend for about 30 seconds, or until very smooth. Serve with a couple of ice cubes, to chill the drink.

GREEN DREAM

Melon and ginger have always made great partners and here kiwi fruit and a dash of lime juice are added to the mix. Top up with chilled, sparkling mineral water after blending, to make a long drink to help you curb your appetite.

Serves 1

¼ ripe honeydew melon
1 ripe kiwi fruit
5ml (1 tsp) grated fresh ginger (see page 3)
10ml (2 tsp) lime juice
75ml (3fl oz) chilled filtered water
ice and chilled sparkling mineral water, to serve

1 Peel, de-seed and roughly chop the melon. Peel and quarter the kiwi fruit. Put the fruit in a blender with the ginger, lime juice and chilled water.
2 Pulse the blender for a few seconds until the fruit is finely chopped, then blend for about 30 seconds until smooth. Pour into a glass with an ice cube or two and top up with sparkling mineral water.

COOK'S TIP
Taste the melon before blending; hopefully it will have a really sweet flavour. If not, reduce the lime juice to 5ml (1 tsp) or you may find the drink too sharp.

MELON, FENNEL AND CUCUMBER COOLER

Staying hydrated is really important if you are trying to lose weight, as the brain often mistakes thirst for hunger. This green-coloured blend is flavoured with fennel, which has a distinct aniseed-like taste that works well with the other ingredients.

Serves 1

¼ **galia melon**
5cm (2in) piece cucumber
25g (1oz) slice fresh fennel
100ml (4fl oz) chilled filtered water

1   Peel and de-seed the melon. Cut the melon, cucumber and fennel into chunks and put in a blender with the water.
2   Pulse the blender for a few seconds until the fruit and vegetables are finely chopped, then blend for about 45 seconds until smooth.

BEACH BLEND

This smoothie has a tropical trio of passion fruit, mango and coconut water, together with yogurt to provide protein and a creamy texture. Mango has a low glycaemic index so will not cause a sudden spike and subsequent fall in blood sugar levels, which can trigger hunger.

Serves 1

1 ripe passion fruit
¼ ripe mango
100ml (4fl oz) low-fat plain bio yogurt
150ml (¼ pint) chilled coconut water
2.5ml (½ tsp) grated fresh ginger (see page 3)
5ml (1 tsp) maca powder (optional)
5ml (1 tsp) ground flaxseed
ice cubes, to serve

1   Halve the passion fruit and scoop out the seeds into a fine sieve placed over a blender. Push the juice and pulp through the sieve into the blender using the back of a spoon and discard the black pips.

2   Peel the mango and roughly chop the flesh. Add to the blender with the yogurt, coconut water, ginger, maca powder if using and ground flaxseed.

3   Blend for about 30 seconds, or until very smooth. Serve with a couple of ice cubes.

BOOZE-FREE PIÑA COLADA

As well as being high in calories, alcohol weakens resolve, so it should be limited if you are trying to lose weight. You can, though, still enjoy all the flavours of this well-known tipple in a healthy drink.

Serves 1

1 small ripe banana
200g (7oz) can pineapple in natural juice
150ml (¼ pint) chilled coconut drinking milk
45ml (3 tbsp) Greek yogurt
ice cubes, to serve

1 Peel the banana and slice or break into smaller pieces. Put in a blender with the pineapple and its juice, coconut milk and yogurt.
2 Pulse the blender for a few seconds, until the banana and pineapple are finely chopped, then blend for about 30 seconds until smooth. Pour into a tall glass and add a couple of ice cubes.

RED PASSION

Packed with red berries, this delicious, brightly coloured blend also contains passion fruit juice, which gives it a slightly exotic flavour. Press the juice out of the seeds, which would give the drink a gritty texture.

Serves 1

1 ripe passion fruit
100g (4oz) fresh or frozen red fruit, such as strawberries, raspberries, cherries and redcurrants
250ml (8fl oz) chilled unsweetened coconut water

1   Halve the passion fruit and scoop out the seeds into a fine sieve. Place over a blender and press out the pulp and juice with the back of a spoon.
2   Wash the red fruit if fresh and add to the blender with the chilled coconut water.
3   Pulse the blender for a few seconds until the fruit is finely chopped, then blend for about 30 seconds, until smooth.

CHOCOLATE CHERRY SMOOTHIE

Here, cherries are combined with raw cacao and skimmed milk to make a healthy drink that will combat those chocolate cravings. Cacao is high in antioxidant flavanoids as well as containing iron and zinc.

Serves 1

75g (3oz) fresh or frozen pitted cherries
15ml (1 tbsp) cacao powder
250ml (8fl oz) chilled skimmed milk
2.5ml (½ tsp) pure vanilla extract
5ml (1 tsp) lacuma powder, honey or agave syrup (optional)

1   Wash the cherries if using fresh and remove the stones (pits). Put the cherries, cacao powder, skimmed milk, vanilla and lacuma powder, honey or agave syrup, if using, in a blender.
2   Pulse the blender for a few seconds until the cherries are finely chopped, then blend for about 30 seconds, until smooth.

BEETROOT AND BLUEBERRY BLAST

Beetroot is one of the best vegetable sources of iron, which is needed for converting food into energy and can be lacking from your diet when you cut back on how much you are eating. Its natural hint of sweetness works well with blueberries in this deep purple drink.

Serves 1

1 small fresh beetroot, about 100g (4oz)
75g (3oz) fresh or frozen blueberries
4 blanched almonds
200ml (7fl oz) chilled unsweetened almond milk

1   Trim the top and root end from the beetroot, then thinly peel and cut into small chunks.
2   Put the beetroot in a blender. If there are any fresh beetroot leaves, wash and add these as well, as they are packed with vitamins. Add the blueberries, almonds and almond milk.
3   Pulse the blender for a few seconds until the beetroot, blueberries and almonds are finely chopped, then blend for about 45 seconds, until smooth.

COOK'S TIP
Beetroot juice can stain your hands and clothes, so take care and either wash immediately after preparation or wear clean rubber gloves.

CHIA SEED, CARROT
AND CUCUMBER COOLER

Chia seeds are a great source of omega-3 fatty acids and also a high-protein food, containing all the essential amino acids. Their ability to swell and absorb liquid makes them a good addition to smoothies when you need a thickener and they are perfect in this filling smoothie.

Serves 1

5ml (1 tsp) chia seeds
100ml (4fl oz) chilled filtered water plus 30ml (2 tbsp) for soaking
1 medium carrot
7.5cm (3in) piece of cucumber
2.5ml (½ tsp) spirulina powder or powdered greens (optional)

1   Put the chia seeds in the blender and add the 30ml (2 tbsp) soaking water. Leave to soak for at least 5 minutes; longer if you have the time. Keep the rest of the water chilled.
2   Peel the carrot and cut the carrot and cucumber into small chunks. Add to the blender with the spirulina powder or powdered greens, if using, and the rest of the water.
3   Pulse the blender for a few seconds until the carrot and cucumber are finely chopped, then blend for about 45 seconds, until fairly smooth.

COOK'S TIP
This blend won't be completely smooth; you will still get tiny flecks of raw carrot.

GRAPES AND GREENS

White seedless grapes and banana add sweetness and texture to this spinach and broccoli blend. It makes a good light lunch or can be served an hour before your evening meal to curb your appetite if you are really hungry in the afternoon.

Serves 1

5ml (1 tsp) chia seeds
175ml (6fl oz) chilled filtered water, plus 15ml (1 tbsp) for soaking
100g (4oz) tenderstem broccoli
100g (4oz) seedless green grapes
½ small ripe banana

1 Put the chia seeds in the blender and add the 15ml (1 tbsp) water. Leave to soak for at least 5 minutes; longer if you have the time. Keep the rest of the water chilled.

2 Wash the broccoli and grapes and peel the banana and cut into slices or break into smaller pieces. Add the broccoli, grapes and banana to the blender.

3 Pulse the blender for a few seconds until the broccoli and fruit are finely chopped, then blend for about 45 seconds until smooth.

COOK'S TIP
Soaking may increase the levels of beneficial ingredients released by chia seeds into the body, so if you remember, soak the seeds in a small covered bowl in the fridge for a few hours or overnight.

APPLE AND SPICE

This apple smoothie is made by blending cooked apple with ground cinnamon, skimmed milk and yogurt. High in protein and calcium, it is excellent served as a mid-morning snack and will keep you energised until lunchtime.

Serves 1

2 green-skinned eating apples
15ml (1 tbsp) water
150ml (¼ pint) chilled skimmed milk
75ml (5 tbsp) low-fat plain bio yogurt
1.5ml (¼ tsp) ground cinnamon
5ml (1 tsp) lecithin granules
5ml (1 tsp) honey, maple syrup or lacuma powder

1 Wash the apples, then quarter them and remove the cores. Cut into smaller chunks and put in a small heatproof bowl with 15ml (1 tbsp) water. Cover with cling film and cook in a microwave on high for 2 minutes. Leave to cool, then chill in the fridge if time allows.
2 Put the apple in a blender with the milk, yogurt, cinnamon, lecithin granules and honey, maple syrup or lacuma powder.
3 Pulse the blender for a few seconds until the apple is finely chopped, then blend for about 30 seconds until smooth and creamy. Serve straight away.

RED HOT

Rooibos (red bush) tea is caffeine-free and rich in antioxidants. Because it contains little tannin it won't impair the body's ability to absorb iron from the beetroot; best of all, it makes a lovely, subtly fruit-flavoured base for this simple smoothie.

Serves 1

1 red-skinned eating apple
1 small beetroot, about 100g (4oz)
5ml (1 tsp) grated fresh ginger (see page 3)
5ml (1 tsp) acai berry powder
200ml (7fl oz) rooibos tea, cooled and chilled

1 Wash the apple, quarter it and remove the core. Top and tail the beetroot and peel thinly. Roughly chop the apple and beetroot and put in a blender.

2 Add the ginger, acai berry powder and chilled tea to the blender.

3 Pulse the blender for a few seconds until the apple and beetroot are finely chopped, then blend for about 45 seconds until smooth.

DRIED FRUIT SALAD SMOOTHIE

Dried fruit is a great source of iron, which is sometimes deficient in women who are dieting or reducing their food intake. Use your favourite combination of dried fruit or a buy a bag of dried mixed 'fruit salad'.

Serves 1

50g (2oz) dried fruit, such as apricots, pears, apples or cranberries
4 blanched almonds
250ml (8fl oz) unsweetened apple juice
100ml (4fl oz) fat-free Greek yogurt

1 Using clean kitchen scissors, snip the fruit into smaller pieces. Put in a bowl, add the almonds, then pour over the apple juice. Cover with cling film and leave to soak in the fridge for at least 2 hours, or preferably overnight.
2 Tip the dried fruit, almonds and juice into a blender and add the yogurt. Pulse the blender for a few seconds until the fruit and almonds are finely chopped, then blend for about 45 seconds until smooth.

FROZEN BERRY AND PINEAPPLE SLUSH

This fruity blend makes an excellent dessert when you want something sweet, but is still healthy and virtually fat-free. Dried skimmed milk is a good source of protein and calcium and adds a creamy taste and texture.

Serves 2

100ml (4fl oz) chilled pineapple juice
10ml (2 tsp) lacuma powder or 5ml (1 tsp) honey
15ml (1 tbsp) dried skimmed milk powder
75g (3oz) frozen strawberries
75g (3oz) frozen pineapple chunks

1 Put the pineapple juice, lacuma powder or honey and skimmed milk powder in a blender. Pulse for a few seconds until just blended.

2 Add the frozen fruit and pulse for about 15 seconds until the fruit is very finely chopped, but not completely smooth. Divide between two glasses and serve with a spoon.

COOK'S TIP
You can buy ready-frozen pineapple, but if you can't find it freeze chunks of fresh or canned pineapple instead.

MANGO, COCONUT AND LIME SMOOTHIE

Among its many health benefits, coconut contains lauric acid, which can help with both weight loss and weight maintenance. Here, coconut drinking milk is combined with juicy mango and a hint of lime.

Serves 1

¼ ripe mango, weighing about 100g (4oz)
250ml (8fl oz) chilled coconut drinking milk
2.5ml (½ tsp) finely grated lime zest
5ml (1 tsp) baobab powder (optional)

1 Peel the mango and cut into chunks. Put in a blender with the coconut drinking milk, lime zest and baobab powder, if using.
2 Pulse the blender for a few seconds until the mango is finely chopped, then blend for about 30 seconds until smooth.

SUPER SKINNY SMOOTHIE

This green smoothie is great at the beginning of a weight-loss diet or when you have over indulged and want to get back on track. It contains pineapple and cucumber, which are both great for detoxifying.

Serves 1

small handful of baby spinach leaves, about 15g (½oz)
5cm (2in) piece cucumber
200g (7oz) can pineapple in natural juice
2.5ml (½ tsp) spirulina or powdered greens
30ml (2 tbsp) filtered water
ice cubes, to serve

1 Wash the spinach, shake dry, then put in a blender. Cut the cucumber into chunks and add with the pineapple and its juice, the spirulina or powdered greens and water.

2 Pulse the blender for a few seconds until the vegetables and pineapple are finely chopped, then blend for about 30 seconds until smooth. Serve with a couple of ice cubes to chill the drink.

FRUIT SALAD AND WHEATGRASS SMOOTHIE

A classic fruit salad contains chopped apples, orange segments, banana slices and a few grapes. It may be a bit old-fashioned but is still a delicious combination. Here it is given a new twist as a smoothie with some added wheatgrass powder for green goodness.

Serves 2

1 orange
1 small eating apple
25g (1oz) seedless red or green grapes
1 small ripe banana
300ml (½ pint) chilled skimmed or semi-skimmed milk
5ml (1 tsp) wheatgrass powder or powdered greens

1　Remove the orange peel with a small sharp knife, cutting off all the white pith. Cut between the membranes to remove the individual segments, discarding any pips. Put the orange segments in a blender and add any juices you can squeeze out of the membranes.

2　Wash the apple and grapes. Quarter and core the apple and add to the blender with the grapes. Peel the banana, then slice or break it into smaller pieces and add that to the blender too. Pour in the milk and add the wheatgrass powder or powdered greens.

3　Pulse the blender for a few seconds until the fruit is finely chopped, then blend for about 30 seconds, until smooth. Divide between two glasses.

SALAD DAYS

If you don't fancy munching your way through a plateful of salad, try turning it into a drink instead. Here, a traditional salad of lettuce, tomatoes and cucumber is blended to make a simple savoury smoothie.

Serves 1

2 vine-ripened tomatoes
50g (2oz) soft lettuce leaves
5cm (2in) piece cucumber
150ml (¼ pint) chilled coconut water
small pinch of salt and freshly ground black pepper
  (optional)

1 Wash the tomatoes and cut into quarters. Wash the lettuce leaves and shake off excess water. Roughly chop the cucumber. Put the vegetables in a blender and pour over the coconut water. Add a small pinch of salt and some freshly ground black pepper, if liked.

2 Pulse the blender for a few seconds, until the vegetables are finely chopped, then blend for about 30 seconds until smooth.

BLUEBERRY PIE

On days when you are desperate for dessert, but want something healthy, this smoothie can fill the gap. It's a rich blend of blueberries, banana and hazelnut milk with just a small amount of kale, flavoured with spice and sweetened with maple syrup.

Serves 1

few kale leaves, about 7g (¼oz)
50g (2oz) fresh or frozen blueberries
1 small ripe banana
10ml (2 tsp) maple syrup
1.5ml (¼ tsp) ground cinnamon
250ml (8fl oz) chilled hazelnut drinking milk

1 Wash the kale and shake off excess water, and the blueberries if using fresh, and put in a blender. Peel the banana and slice or break into smaller pieces. Add to the blender with the maple syrup, cinnamon and hazelnut milk.
2 Pulse the blender for a few seconds until the kale and fruit are finely chopped, then blend for about 30 seconds until smooth.

SUMMER FRUIT AND DANDELION GREENS

Made with fresh peaches and raspberries and scented with lavender, this smoothie makes the most of 'free' dandelion leaves – a natural diuretic, which encourages the body to break down fat.

Serves 1

1 stem of lavender flowers
6 small or 4 medium young dandelion leaves
75ml (3fl oz) boiling water
1 ripe peach
25g (1oz) fresh or frozen raspberries
150ml (¼ pint) chilled almond milk

1 Rinse the lavender and dandelion leaves under cold running water, then shake off the excess water. Put the dandelion leaves to one side then break the flowery top of the lavender from the stem and put in a heatproof bowl. Pour over 75ml (3fl oz) boiling water, cover and leave to infuse. When cool, chill in the fridge for about 15 minutes.

2 Put the peach in a heatproof bowl and pour over enough boiling water to cover. Leave for 1 minute, then lift out with a slotted spoon and rinse under cold water. Peel off the skin, halve the peach and remove the stone. Roughly chop the flesh and put in a blender with the dandelion leaves, raspberries and almond milk. Strain in the lavender water, discarding the flowers.

3 Pulse the blender for a few seconds until the fruit and dandelion leaves are finely chopped, then blend for about 30 seconds until smooth.

> **COOK'S TIP**
> It is essential that you use unsprayed dandelion leaves and lavender flowers. If you have the slightest doubt, don't pick them, as even in the countryside nearby fields may have been sprayed. The best source is from your own garden, making sure you double-check with whoever does the gardening that the flowers and leaves are untreated.

BERRY BANANA SOYA MILK SMOOTHIE

Bananas and berries are both excellent sources of potassium, which can help promote weight loss. Here they are combined with soya milk – a great alternative to dairy milk, as it has a creamy taste but is lower in sugar.

Serves 1

75g (3oz) mixed fresh or frozen berries, such as strawberries, raspberries, blackcurrants or blackberries
1 small ripe banana
200ml (7fl oz) chilled unsweeteened soya milk
5ml (1 tsp) acai berry powder (optional)

1 Wash the berries if using fresh and put in a blender. Peel the banana and slice or break into smaller pieces. Add to the blender with the soya milk and acai berry powder, if using.
2 Pulse the blender for a few seconds until the fruit is finely chopped, then blend for about 30 seconds until smooth.

CLEMENTINE AND MANGO SMOOTHIE

This is a great way to use up some of those clementines or similar citrus fruit in the fruit bowl during the winter months, when it becomes harder to stick to a healthy diet. It's great to serve for breakfast if you have eaten to excess during the festive season.

Serves 2

8 clementines
1 small mango
1 small ripe banana
150ml (¼ pint) low-fat bio yogurt
10ml (2 tsp) acai berry powder (optional)
ice cubes to serve

1 Halve the clementines and squeeze out all the juice; there should be about 300ml (½ pint). Pour the juice into a blender, discarding any pips.
2 Slice the mango lengthwise on either side of the stone. Peel and roughly chop the flesh, discarding the stone. Peel the banana and slice or break into pieces. Add the mango, banana and yogurt to the blender. Add the acai berry powder, if using.
3 Pulse the blender for a few seconds until the fruit is finely chopped, then blend for about 30 seconds until smooth. Pour into 2 glasses, adding ice cubes, to chill the drink.

GRAPE ESCAPE

Grapes with red and black skins have antioxidant properties, as they are high in bioflavonoids. These are passed on when making red wine, which is why many consider a daily glass is good for you. As alcohol should be limited on a calorie-controlled diet, this fresh grape blend is a better choice.

Serves 1

100g (4oz) red seedless grapes
1 small ripe banana
175ml (6fl oz) chilled skimmed or semi-skimmed milk
5ml (1 tsp) lecithin granules

1 Wash the grapes and remove any stalks. Peel the banana and slice or break into smaller pieces. Put the fruit in a blender with the milk and lecithin granules.
2 Pulse the blender for a few seconds until the fruit is finely chopped, then blend for about 45 seconds until fairly smooth.

COOK'S TIP
The grape skins won't blend completely smooth, making this a slightly speckled blend.

PINK GRAPEFRUIT AND PINEAPPLE PICK-ME-UP

Grapefruit has always been associated with low-calorie diets, but the yellow variety can be very acidic. Pink grapefruit has a sweeter flavour and stunning colour and as well as being packed with vitamin C, contains the antioxidant beta-carotene, which is converted into vitamin A by the body.

Serves 1

1 pink or ruby grapefruit
¼ ripe pineapple, about 200g (7oz) flesh, once skin and
**   core have been removed**
150ml (¼ pint) chilled pineapple juice
ice cubes, to serve

1   Working over a bowl to catch the juice, peel the grapefruit, removing all the bitter white pith, then cut it into segments between the membranes, removing any pips. Place in a blender.
2   Roughly chop the pineapple and add to the blender. Pour over the pineapple juice.
3   Pulse the blender for a few seconds until the fruit is finely chopped, then blend for about 30 seconds until smooth. When serving, add a couple of ice cubes to the glass to chill the drink.

CASHEW NUT MILK WITH GREENS

Cashews are soft, so don't need long soaking like many other nuts to blend them into creamy milk. In this drink, dates are added to both sweeten and thicken and a few greens make this a rich and satisfying smoothie.

Serves 1

75g (3oz) raw cashews
2 ready-to-eat pitted dried dates, such as Medjool
200ml (7fl oz) chilled filtered water
small handful of baby spinach leaves, about 15g (½oz)
small pinch of salt (optional)

1 Put the cashews in a blender with the dates and pour over the water. Wash the spinach leaves and shake off the excess water. Add to the blender with a small pinch of salt, if liked.
2 Pulse the blender for a few seconds until the nuts, dates and spinach are finely chopped, then blend for about 45 seconds until very smooth.

TROPICAL COLADA

Coconut milk can be beneficial for losing and maintaining weight, and combining it with paypaya and pineapple makes a deliciously exotic-tasting drink. This recipe makes enough to share, cheers!

Serves 2

1 ripe papaya (pawpaw)
¼ ripe pineapple, about 200g (7oz) flesh, once skin and
  core have been removed
300ml (½ pint) chilled coconut drinking milk
5ml (1 tsp) baobab (optional)
ice cubes, to serve

1 Cut the papaya in half, scoop out the black seeds and discard. Thinly peel, then chop the flesh and put it in a blender. Roughly chop the pineapple and add with the coconut drinking milk and baobab, if using.

2 Pulse the blender for a few seconds until the fruit is finely chopped, then blend for about 30 seconds until smooth. Add ice cubes to two glasses and divide the smoothie between them.

FOREST FRUIT SMOOTHIE

Blackberries are the richest fruit source of vitamin E and are very low in calories. If you pick your own in autumn, freeze them in small batches to make this smoothie during the winter months; the pips don't break down completely when blended, but this adds plenty of fibre to the drink.

Serves 1

100g (4oz) fresh or frozen blackberries
10ml (2 tsp) rosehip syrup
200ml (7fl oz) chilled hazelnut drinking milk
5ml (1 tsp) wheat germ

1   Wash the blackberries if fresh and put in a blender with the rosehip syrup, hazelnut milk and wheat germ.
2   Pulse the blender for a few seconds until the blackberries are finely chopped, then blend for about 30 seconds until fairly smooth.

MANGO, ORANGE AND WATERCRESS SMOOTHIE

Iron is often lacking when you are trying to reduce your food intake and a deficiency can leave you feeling tired and lacking concentration. Watercress is a great vegetable source of iron and the vitamin C in the fruit will help your body to absorb this so that none is wasted.

Serves 2

1 ripe mango
1 bunch of watercress
300ml (½ pint) chilled orange juice or a mixture of orange
  juice and filtered water
ice cubes, to serve

1 Slice the mango either side of the stone, then peel and roughly chop the flesh. Put in a blender.

2 Wash the watercress and shake off excess water, then cut off the bottom half of the stalks and discard. Put the leaves and top half of the stalks into the blender. Pour over the orange juice.

3 Pulse the blender for a few seconds or until the mango and watercress are finely chopped, then blend for about 30 seconds until smooth. Put a few ice cubes in two glasses and divide the smoothie between them.

STRAWBERRY AND MELON JUICE

Even if you eat a healthy diet and exercise regularly, if you do not drink enough liquid you will not burn fat efficiently. This is because when the body perceives thirst, its processes and metabolism slow down. This blend is excellent for keeping you hydrated.

Serves 2

100g (4oz) fresh or frozen strawberries
½ ripe melon, such as honeydew or cantaloupe
freshly squeezed juice of ½ lime
45ml (3 tbsp) filtered water
ice cubes, to serve

1 Wash and hull the strawberries, if fresh. Cut any large ones in half and put them in a blender. Cut the melon in quarters and scoop out the seeds, then cut the flesh away from the rind and roughly chop. Add to the blender with the lime juice and water.
2 Pulse the blender for a few seconds until the fruit is finely chopped, then blend for about 30 seconds until smooth.
3 Divide between two glasses, adding a few ice cubes to chill the drink.

SPICED PEACH AND ALMOND SMOOTHIE

Although peaches are available all year round, their true season is relatively short, so make the most of them while they are at their best and least expensive. They are low in calories and packed with antioxidants and flavour.

Serves 1

2 ripe fresh peaches
25g (1oz) flaked almonds
150ml (¼ pint) chilled filtered water
pinch of ground cinnamon
pinch of ground ginger
5ml (1 tsp) honey, maple syrup or agave syrup

1 Put the peaches in a heatproof bowl and pour over just enough boiling water to cover. Leave for 1 minute, then remove and rinse under cold water. Peel the peaches (the skins should slide off easily), halve them and remove the stones, then roughly chop the flesh.

2 Put the peaches, almonds, water, cinnamon, ginger and honey, maple syrup or agave syrup in a blender.

3 Pulse the blender for a few seconds until the fruit and almonds are finely chopped, then blend for about 30 seconds until smooth.

BANANA AND CHERRY SMOOTHIE

Bananas may contain a few more calories than other fruit, but they are filling and nutritious and make fantastically thick and creamy smoothies. Here they are combined with cherries to make a delicious and attractive drink.

Serves 1

1 small ripe banana
50g (2oz) fresh or frozen pitted cherries
250ml (8fl oz) chilled skimmed milk or unsweetened
  almond milk
5ml (1 tsp) baobab powder (optional)

1   Peel the banana and slice or break it into smaller pieces. If using fresh, wash the cherries before pitting. Put the banana and cherries in a blender with the milk and baobab powder, if using.

2   Pulse the blender for a few seconds until the fruit is finely chopped, then blend for about 30 seconds until smooth.

GOOD AND GREEN

This fruit and vegetable blend is not only very low in calories but is really good for you, providing lots of vitamins and minerals and keeping you well hydrated.

Serves 1

large handful of baby spinach leaves, about 25g (1oz)
1 green-skinned eating apple
1 green-skinned ripe pear
¼ cucumber
150ml (¼ pint) chilled filtered water

1   Wash the spinach leaves and shake off the excess water. Wash the apple and pear, quarter them and remove the cores. Roughly chop into smaller pieces with the cucumber. Put the fruit and vegetables in a blender with the water.
2   Pulse the blender for a few seconds until everything is finely chopped, then blend for about 45 seconds until smooth.

SWEET DREAMS

There's nothing worse than going to bed feeling hungry; this soothing, high-carbohydrate smoothie made with banana, oat milk, cinnamon and nutmeg served half an hour or so before bedtime will help get you to sleep.

Serves 1

1 small ripe banana
200ml (7fl oz) chilled oat milk
5ml (1 tsp) honey or agave syrup
pinch of ground cinnamon
pinch of freshly grated nutmeg

1   Peel the banana and slice or break into smaller pieces. Put in a blender with the milk, honey or agave syrup, cinnamon and most of the nutmeg.
2   Blend for about 30 seconds until smooth, then pour into a glass and sprinkle over the rest of the nutmeg.

3
EXERCISE ENHANCERS

MELLOW MORNING

Barleygrass is slightly easier to digest than wheatgrass and other powdered greens and has a milder flavour that you may prefer. It can be useful after exercise as it reduces inflammation in the body.

Serves 1

¼ ripe honeydew melon
1 small ripe banana
5ml (1 tsp) finely grated lime zest, plus 5ml (1 tsp) lime juice
5ml (1 tsp) honey
5ml (1 tsp) barleygrass powder
200ml (7fl oz) chilled semi-skimmed milk
ice cubes, to serve

1   Scoop the seeds out of the melon and discard. Peel the melon and banana and cut into chunks. Put into a blender with the lime zest and juice, honey, barleygrass powder and milk.
2   Blend for about 30 seconds until well blended and smooth. Put one or two ice cubes in a glass and pour over the smoothie.

AVOCADO AND ALMOND SMOOTHIE

This vibrant green creamy drink has a gorgeous nutty flavour from both the almonds and tahini. Avocados are fairly high in fat, but this is the 'good for you' monounsaturated variety and they are full of other beneficial nutrients too, such as potassium.

Serves 1

½ ripe avocado
2 ready-to-eat pitted dates, such as Medjool
4 blanched almonds
small handful of baby spinach leaves, about 15g (½oz)
5ml (1 tsp) tahini paste
250ml (8fl oz) chilled almond milk

1 Remove the skin and stone from the avocado, roughly chop the flesh and put in a blender. Add the stones to the blender with the almonds, spinach leaves, tahini and almond milk.

2 Pulse the blender for a few seconds until the dates, almonds and spinach are finely chopped, then blend for about 45 seconds until smooth.

BANANA NUT SHAKE

Peanut butter is high in protein so is great for bodybuilders. It adds a subtle nutty flavour and creaminess to this shake, which is made with skimmed milk to reduce the fat content a little.

Serves 1

1 small ripe banana
30ml (2 tbsp) smooth peanut butter
200ml (7fl oz) chilled skimmed milk

1 Peel the banana and slice or break into smaller pieces. Put in a blender, add the peanut butter, then pour in the milk.
2 Pulse the blender for a few seconds until the banana is finely chopped, then blend for about 30 seconds until smooth.

PEAR, DATE AND ALMOND RESTORER

This is a great energy booster before or after exercise or at any time of the day when you need a lift. Flaxseed is a natural source of omega-3, which is good for both your heart and joints.

Serves 1

1 ripe pear
2 ready-to-eat pitted dates, such as Medjool
10ml (2 tsp) ground flaxseed
175ml (6fl oz) chilled unsweetened almond milk

1   Wash the pear, quarter it and remove the core, then put it in a blender. Add the dates, ground flaxseed and almond milk.
2   Pulse the blender for a few seconds until the pear and dates are finely chopped, then blend for about 30 seconds until smooth.

BONE BUILDER

Tofu, tahini and milk are all great sources of calcium, which is essential for building and maintaining bones. It can also help weight loss, as a good supply of calcium suppresses the hormone calcitriol, which is responsible for increasing fat stores in the body.

Serves 1

75g (3oz) silken tofu
10ml (2 tsp) tahini
2 Brazil nuts
5ml (1 tsp) sunflower seeds
200ml (7fl oz) chilled skimmed milk
2.5ml (½ tsp) pure vanilla extract

1   Put the tofu, tahini, Brazil nuts, sunflower seeds, skimmed milk and vanilla extract in a blender.
2   Pulse the blender for a few seconds until the nuts and seeds are finely chopped, then blend on high for about 45 seconds until smooth.

BODY BUILDER

This high-carbohydrate, high-protein drink is ideal before strenuous exercise or as a meal replacement. It includes soya protein powder, but you could use hemp protein powder if you prefer.

Serves 1

1 small ripe banana
1 ripe pear
150ml (¼ pint) chilled coconut drinking milk
15ml (1 tbsp) skimmed milk powder
15ml (1 tbsp) soya protein powder
5ml (1 tsp) ground flaxseed
5ml (1 tsp) sunflower seeds
ice cubes, to serve

1 Peel the banana and slice or break it into smaller pieces. Wash the pear, quarter it and remove the core. Put the banana and pear in a blender with the coconut drinking milk, skimmed milk powder, protein powder, ground flaxseed and sunflower seeds.

2 Pulse the blender for a few seconds until the fruit and seeds are finely chopped, then blend for about 30 seconds until smooth. Pour into a glass and add a couple of ice cubes to chill the drink.

WATERMELON AND STRAWBERRY SLUSHIE

Hydrating, low in calories and with a high glycaemic index, watermelon is a good choice after exercise to refuel muscles. Freeze in chunks a few hours before you need it and blend with strawberries to make a delicious, semi-frozen fruit treat.

Serves 1

1 large wedge of watermelon, or half a 'baby' watermelon, about 250g (9oz) flesh in total
50g (2oz) fresh or frozen strawberries
few drops of rose water (optional)

1   Cut the watermelon flesh into chunks, discarding any large, hard pips, and place in a freezer container. Cover and freeze for at least 3 hours, or overnight if preferred.
2   Wash and hull the strawberries, if using fresh. Put in the blender with the watermelon and a few drops of rose water, if liked.
3   Pulse the blender for a few seconds until the strawberries are finely chopped, then blend for about 45 seconds or until the mixture is smooth. Tip into a chilled glass.

COOK'S TIP
If you are using frozen strawberries, only freeze the watermelon for an hour, so that the fruit is not all completely frozen. This makes the resulting drink easier to blend and nicer to drink.

WATERMELON AND CRANBERRY QUENCHER

Use sweetened dried cranberries for this drink; they are simply too tart without sugar! They add an intense and refreshing taste to this bright, reddish-pink smoothie, which won't just quench your thirst, but is packed with vitamin C to boost your immune system, too.

Serves 1

1 large wedge of watermelon, or half a 'baby' watermelon, about 250g (9oz) flesh in total
25g (1oz) sweetened dried cranberries
5ml (1 tsp) acai berry powder (optional)
200ml (7fl oz) chilled coconut water
ice cubes, to serve

1   Cut the watermelon into chunks, discarding any large, hard pips. Put the fruit in a blender with the dried cranberries, acai berry powder, if using, and coconut water.

2   Pulse the blender for a few seconds until the watermelon and cranberries are finely chopped, then blend for about 30 seconds until smooth. Pour into a glass, adding a couple of ice cubes to chill the drink.

APRICOT, ALMOND AND PINEAPPLE BLEND

Dried apricots are a very rich source of beta-carotene and contain both iron and potassium, both of which make them ideal for a post-exercise snack. This smoothie will help to boost energy levels and refuel tired muscles.

Serves 1

75g (3oz) ready-to-eat dried apricots
5 blanched almonds
150ml (¼ pint) pineapple juice
150ml (¼ pint) filtered water

1   Roughly chop the apricots and put them in the blender cup or a bowl with the almonds, pineapple juice and water. If using a blender cup, screw on the top. If using a bowl, cover with cling film. Leave to soak in the fridge overnight.
2   If soaking in a bowl, tip the mixture into the blender. Pulse the blender for a few seconds or until the apricots and almonds are finely chopped, then blend for about a minute or until smooth.

COOK'S TIP
The apricots and almonds are best soaked overnight, as the long soaking makes a lovely smooth and creamy drink, but a couple of hours' soaking is sufficient if you're in a rush – you could put the ingredients together before you head out for your workout, then blitz them when you get back.

APRICOT SMOOTHIE

Don't overlook canned fruit; it often contains as many nutrients as fresh, although you should try to select fruit packed in natural juice rather than sugary syrup. Here, canned apricots are combined with apricot yogurt and ice-cold almond milk, making a quick and easy, calcium-rich drink.

Serves 1

200g (7oz) can apricots in natural juice
125g (5oz) carton good-quality apricot yogurt, or plain bio yogurt, if you prefer
about 150ml (5fl oz) chilled almond milk

1 Tip the apricots and juice into a blender (there's no need to chop the apricots first). Add the yogurt and about two-thirds of the almond milk.
2 Blend for 30–45 seconds until very smooth. Check the consistency; this will vary depending on how much juice was in the can. If you prefer a thinner consistency, add the rest of the almond milk and blend for a few more seconds. Serve immediately.

PEACH AND ORANGE SMOOTHIE

Using canned fruit in natural juice is one of the simplest ways of making a smoothie, especially if you are in a hurry and don't want to spend time preparing fresh fruit. Here, peaches are combined with a little orange juice and a carton of fruit yogurt to make a quick and nutritious drink.

Serves 1

200g (7oz) can peaches in natural juice
125g (5oz) carton good-quality peach yogurt, or plain bio yogurt, if you prefer
150ml (¼ pint) chilled unsweetened orange juice

1 Put the peaches and their juice, yogurt and orange juice in a blender.
2 Pulse the blender for a few seconds until the peaches are finely chopped, then blend for about 30 seconds until smooth.

BLUEBERRY AND PINEAPPLE BLEND

Immediately after exercise you may not feel like eating, so drinking a smoothie is a fast way to restore energy levels and reduce tiredness. Fruit yogurt adds flavour but does contain a little sugar, so you may prefer to use plain bio yogurt here instead.

Serves 1

150g (5oz) fresh or frozen blueberries
150g (5oz) pineapple or coconut-flavoured yogurt
150ml (¼ pint) chilled pineapple juice
ice cubes, to serve

1   If using fresh blueberries, rinse them in a sieve under cold running water. Drain well and tip into the blender. Add the yogurt and pineapple juice.
2   Pulse the blender for a few seconds or until the fruit is finely chopped, then blend for 30–45 seconds or until smooth. Pour into a glass and add a couple of ice cubes, if liked, to chill the drink.

FRESH PLUM AND APPLE SMOOTHIE

Plentiful in minerals such as potassium, iron and fluoride, plums have a lovely sweet and slightly tart flavour. Here they are blended with apple, carrot and spinach to make a nourishing green smoothie; great after a workout or when you are feeling tired in the afternoon.

Serves 1

2 ripe plums, preferably yellow
1 green eating apple
1 small carrot
small handful of fresh baby spinach leaves, about 15g (½oz)
150ml (¼ pint) chilled filtered water

1   Wash the plums and apple, then halve the plums and remove the stones. Quarter the apple and remove the core and pips. Top, tail and peel the carrot. Roughly chop the plums, apple and carrot and put in the blender. Wash the spinach leaves and shake off excess water, then add to the blender.

2   Add the water, then pulse the blender for a few seconds until the fruit and vegetables are finely chopped. Blend for a minute or until completely smooth.

3   Check the consistency of the smoothie and add a little more water if you prefer it thinner, then briefly blend again.

COOK'S TIP
You can use any plum variety for this smoothie, but yellow ones are higher in vitamin A and beta-carotene than purple ones, and also make this smoothie a more attractive colour.

SPICED PRUNE AND APPLE SMOOTHIE

Prunes are rich in carbohydrate and iron, so make a great post-exercise smoothie, and combined with a little Greek yogurt, they can be turned into a delicious, creamy drink. The vitamin C in apple juice will help the body to absorb the iron. Don't drink this before you exercise, as prunes are well known for their laxative effect.

Serves 1

75g (3oz) ready-to-eat pitted prunes
1.5ml (¼ tsp) ground cinnamon
pinch of ground ginger
300ml (½ pint) apple juice
30ml (2 tbsp) Greek yogurt

1 Roughly chop the prunes and put in the blender cup or a bowl with the cinnamon, ginger and apple juice. If using a blender cup, screw on the top. If using a bowl, cover with cling film. Leave to soak in the fridge for at least 3 hours, or overnight if preferred.

2 If soaking in a bowl, tip the mixture into the blender. Add the yogurt and pulse the blender for a few seconds or until the prunes are finely chopped, then blend for about a minute or until smooth.

STRAWBERRY AND REDCURRANT BLITZ

High in antioxidants, vitamins C and E and carotene, redcurrants contain significant amounts of calcium and iron. But the redcurrant season is relatively short, so make sure you freeze some of these vibrant red berries for smoothie-making during the rest of the year. As they have a tart flavour, combine them with really ripe sweet strawberries to make them more palatable.

Serves 1

100g (4oz) fresh strawberries
100g (4oz) fresh or frozen redcurrants
Freshly squeezed juice of 1 orange
150ml (¼ pint) filtered water, chilled if using fresh rather than frozen fruit
5–10ml (1–2 tsp) agave syrup or clear honey

1   Wash and hull the strawberries. If using fresh redcurrants, rinse under cold running water, then remove the berries from the sprigs using the tines of a fork.
2   Put the fruit in a blender and add the orange juice, water, agave syrup or honey.
3   Pulse the blender for a few seconds or until the fruit is finely chopped, then blend for 30–45 seconds or until smooth.

SUMMER FRUIT SIPPER

Fluid intake is important, especially during the hot summer months, and more so during and after exercise. Cooled and chilled fruit tea makes a great base for this thirst-quenching smoothie.

Serves 1

1 red fruit tea bag
few fresh mint leaves
about 250ml (8fl oz) near-boiling filtered water (a mugful)
1 large wedge of watermelon, or half a 'baby' watermelon,
   about 250g (9oz) flesh in total
50g (2oz) fresh or frozen strawberries

1 Put the teabag and mint leaves in a heatproof jug or mug and pour over the near-boiling water. Leave to steep for 5 minutes, then remove the teabag and mint, leave to cool, then chill in the fridge.

2 Cut the watermelon flesh into chunks, discarding any large hard pips. Wash the strawberries, if using fresh, and hull them. Put the watermelon and strawberries in a blender and pour in the chilled fruit and mint tea.

3 Pulse the blender for a few seconds until the fruit is finely chopped, then blend for about 30 seconds until smooth.

GREEN GODDESS

Vitamin C is vital when exercising as it helps protect against muscle damage, reduces soreness and promotes healing. Weight for weight, kiwi fruit are higher in vitamin C than oranges and their flavour works well with mellow pears and stronger-tasting kale.

Serves 1

1 ripe pear
2 ripe kiwi fruit
large handful of kale, about 25g (1oz)
175ml (6fl oz) chilled coconut water or a mixture of
  coconut water and filtered water

1 Wash the pear, quarter and remove the core. Thinly peel the kiwi fruit and cut into quarters. Wash the kale and shake off excess water. Put the fruit and kale in a blender and pour over the coconut water or filtered water.
2 Pulse the blender for a few seconds until the fruit and kale are finely chopped, then blend for about 45 seconds until fairly smooth. Serve straight away.

FIG AND BANANA SOYA SMOOTHIE

Bananas are great for carbohydrate-loading and here they are combined with fresh fig, soya milk and camu-camu, which is good for banishing fatigue. Enjoy this drink before, during or after exercise.

Serves 1

1 fresh ripe fig
1 medium or large ripe banana
250ml (8fl oz) chilled unsweetened soya milk
5ml (1 tsp) camu-camu (optional)

1 Carefully wash the fig then cut it into quarters and put in a blender. Peel the banana and slice or break it into smaller pieces. Add to the blender with the soya milk and camu-camu, if using.
2 Pulse the blender for a few seconds until the fig and banana are finely chopped, then blend for about 30 seconds until smooth. Serve straight away.

PASSION FRUIT AND COCONUT ICE

You'll need a powerful blender to crush ice, but it does make a lovely base for rich smoothies and quickly cools drinks on hot days. Use no more than 5 or 6 ice cubes, though, or you will dilute the blend too much.

Serves 1

5–6 ice cubes
1 ripe passion fruit
200ml (7fl oz) chilled coconut drinking milk
5ml (1 tsp) baobab powder (optional)

1   Crush the ice cubes in a blender, tip into a chilled glass and leave in the fridge while making the smoothie.
2   Halve the passion fruit and scoop out the seeds into a fine sieve placed over the blender. Press with the back of a spoon to extract all the pulp and juice, then discard the seeds. Pour the coconut milk into the blender and sprinkle over the baobab powder, if using.
3   Blend for about 15 seconds until smooth, then pour over the crushed ice and serve straight away.

GRAPE AND GOJI BERRY BLEND

Goji berries are high in vitamins B1 and B2, calcium, iron, selenium and phosphorous, so give a nutritional boost to this hydrating blend. The natural sugars in grapes aid recovery after moderate or strenuous exercise.

Serves 1

15ml (1 tbsp) dried goji berries
200ml (7fl oz) filtered water, chilled if using fresh rather than frozen blueberries
1 eating apple
100g (4oz) seedless green grapes
75g (3oz) fresh or frozen blueberries

1   Put the goji berries in a blender and pour over the water. Leave to soak for a few minutes while preparing the rest of the fruit.
2   Wash the apple, quarter and core it. Wash the grapes and the blueberries, if using fresh. Add the fruit to the blender.
3   Pulse the blender for a few seconds until the fruit is finely chopped, then blend for about 45 seconds until smooth. Serve straight away.

MINTY CUCUMBER LASSI

This easily absorbed isotonic drink is based on the Indian drink lassi, which is usually either very sweet or salty. This version is sugar-free, but you can add a little salt if you like, as it intensifies the flavour and can be useful after exercise.

Serves 1

½ cucumber, about 200g (7oz)
200ml (7fl oz) plain bio yogurt
75ml (3fl oz) chilled skimmed milk
3–4 small mint leaves
small pinch of ground cumin (optional)
small pinch of salt (optional)
ice cubes, to serve

1   Wash the cucumber, cut in half lengthways and scoop out and discard the seeds. Roughly chop the flesh and put in a blender with the yogurt, milk, mint leaves and cumin and salt, if using.
2   Pulse the blender for a few seconds until the cucumber is finely chopped, then blend for about 30 seconds until smooth. Pour into a glass, adding a couple of ice cubes to chill the drink.

TROPICAL TREAT

This satisfying smoothie is a good source of protein and calcium, so it's great for building muscles and for promoting bone health and strength. For a smoother drink, soak the nuts for a few hours before use.

Serves 1

½ ripe mango
1 small ripe banana
100ml (4fl oz) plain bio yogurt
150ml (¼ pint) chilled unsweetened pineapple juice
2 blanched almonds
1 whole Brazil nut

1 Peel the mango and roughly cut off the flesh around the stone. Peel the banana and slice or break it into smaller pieces. Put the fruit in a blender with the yogurt, pineapple juice and nuts.

2 Pulse the blender for a few seconds until the fruit and nuts are finely chopped, then blend for about 45 seconds until smooth.

COOK'S TIP
If time allows, put the nuts in a jug with the pineapple juice, cover and leave to soak in the fridge for 3–4 hours, or overnight; this will soften the nuts and make a smoother-textured drink.

LUNCH-TO-GO

Tofu is especially useful for vegans and vegetarians as a source of protein. Silken tofu makes smoothies thick and creamy and, combined with nuts, seeds and some fresh fruit, it makes a highly nutritious liquid lunch.

Serves 1

50g (2oz) fresh or frozen strawberries
75g (3oz) silken tofu
10ml (2 tsp) pumpkin seeds
5ml (1 tsp) honey or agave syrup
200ml (7fl oz) chilled semi-skimmed milk or unsweetened
  soya milk
5ml (1 tsp) barleygrass powder (optional)

1 Rinse the strawberries if fresh, hull, then put them in a blender with the tofu, pumpkin seeds, honey or agave syrup, milk and barleygrass powder, if using.
2 Blend for a few seconds until the strawberries and seeds are finely chopped, then blend for about 30 seconds until smooth. Serve straight away.

COOK'S TIP
Firm silken tofu comes in small cartons and is an unpressed tofu with a soft crumbly texture. Once opened, tip the rest of the tofu into a sealable container and store in the fridge for up to 3 days.

GREEN PROTEIN SMOOTHIE

High in protein, this is a great smoothie after moderate to strenuous exercise and will help to build muscles. Hazelnuts and hazelnut milk add a lovely flavour too, so that the spirulina doesn't overpower the drink.

Serves 1

1 small ripe banana
25g (1oz) skinned hazelnuts
250ml (8fl oz) chilled hazelnut milk
30ml (2 tbsp) Greek yogurt
15ml (1 tbsp) soya protein powder
5ml (1 tsp) spirulina or powdered greens

1   Peel the banana and slice or break it into smaller pieces. Put in a blender with the hazelnuts, hazelnut milk, yogurt, protein powder and spirulina or powdered greens.

2   Pulse the blender for a few seconds until the banana and nuts are finely chopped, then blend for about 30 seconds until smooth.

COOK'S TIP
If you prefer, use blanched almonds and almond milk instead of hazelnuts and hazelnut milk.

GREEN FRUIT BLEND

Vitamin C is particularly useful when exercising as it reduces muscle soreness and speeds up healing. If you are not a great fan of citrus fruit, try this kiwi fruit alternative; kiwis contain more vitamin C than the equivalent weight of oranges.

Serves 1

1 ripe pear
2 ripe kiwi fruit
150ml (¼ pint) chilled filtered water
5ml (1 tsp) honey or agave syrup
5ml (1 tsp) lime juice
2.5ml (½ tsp) baobab powder (optional)
ice cubes, to serve

1 Wash the pear, then quarter, core and put it in a blender. Thinly peel the kiwi fruit and roughly chop. Add to the blender with the water, honey or agave syrup, lime juice and baobab powder, if using.
2 Pulse the blender for a few seconds until the fruit is finely chopped, then blend for about 30 seconds until smooth. Pour into a glass, adding a couple of ice cubes to chill the drink.

CREAMY DATE AND MACADAMIA SMOOTHIE

This is perfect as an energy-giving snack after a workout or to give you a boost mid-afternoon on a busy day. Macadamia nuts are rich in the B-vitamin complex, vitamin E, potassium and calcium. They are also rich in monounsaturated fat and give this smoothie a rich and silky texture.

Serves 1

4 ready-to-eat pitted dried dates, such as Medjool
5 macadamia nuts
60ml (4 tbsp) filtered water
250ml (8fl oz) chilled unsweetened almond milk
5ml (1 tsp) ground flaxseed (optional)
5ml (1 tsp) maca powder (optional)
2.5ml (½ tsp) pure vanilla extract

1 Put the dates and nuts in a small bowl and spoon over 60ml (4 tbsp) filtered water. Cover and leave to soak in the fridge for at least 4 hours, or overnight if preferred.
2 Tip the dates and nuts and their soaking liquid into a blender. Add the almond milk, flaxseed and maca powder, if using, and vanilla extract.
3 Pulse the blender for a few seconds until the dates and nuts are finely chopped, then blend for about 45 seconds until smooth.

COOK'S TIP
If you prefer, use the seeds from a vanilla pod rather than vanilla extract. Cut a vanilla pod in half, then split one half open lengthways using the tip of a sharp knife (keep the other uncut half for another recipe). Scrape out the tiny black seeds and add to the blender with the dates and nuts.

SUNSHINE SEED SMOOTHIE

Seeds are nutritional powerhouses and are packed with vitamins, notably the antioxidant vitamin E, and minerals, particularly iron and oils that are great for maintaining healthy joints.

Serves 1

½ ripe mango
2.5ml (½ tsp) finely grated orange zest
30ml (2 tbsp) sunflower seeds
15ml (1 tbsp) pumpkins seeds
10ml (2 tsp) sesame seeds
250ml (8fl oz) chilled unsweetened rice milk

1 Cut the mango flesh into chunks and put it in a blender with the orange zest, seeds and rice milk.
2 Pulse the blender for a few seconds until the mango and seeds are finely chopped, then blend for about 45 seconds until smooth. Serve straight away.

BLACKBERRY AND APPLE BLEND

After the glut of summer fruit, blackberries make a welcome arrival, not least because they can be collected from the hedgerows for free! Once picked, they don't keep well, so freeze your harvest in small batches for future smoothies – they make a nice change from other fruits and are rich in antioxidants, too.

Serves 1

100g (4oz) fresh or frozen blackberries
200ml (7fl oz) chilled unsweetened apple juice
45ml (3 tbsp) fromage frais

1 Wash the blackberries if fresh and put in a blender. Add the apple juice and fromage frais.
2 Pulse the blender for a few seconds until the blackberries are finely chopped, then blend for about 30 seconds until smooth.

AUTUMN FRUIT SMOOTHIE

Blackberries are packed with antioxidants and work well with other seasonal fruit, such as plums and pears. Here they are blended with hazelnuts and hazelnut milk, which boosts the calcium and protein content of the drink, but you can use dairy milk and different nuts, if you prefer.

Serves 1

100g (4oz) fresh or frozen blackberries
1 ripe pear
1 ripe plum
200ml (7fl oz) chilled hazelnut milk
25g (1oz) skinned hazelnuts

1 Wash the blackberries if fresh, the pear and plum. Quarter and core the pear and halve the plum and remove the stone. Put the prepared fruit in a blender with the hazelnut milk and hazelnuts.

2 Pulse the blender for a few seconds until the fruit and nuts are finely chopped, then blend for about 45 seconds until smooth. Serve straight away.

SAVOURY TOMATO SMOOTHIE

This smoothie has the concentrated flavour of sun-dried tomatoes, which contain a range of antioxidants and B vitamins that are essential for converting food to energy to see you through a tough workout. Make sure you select ordinary sun-dried tomatoes rather than those preserved in oil.

Serves 1

4 sun-dried tomatoes
25g (1oz) blanched almonds
150ml (¼ pint) boiling water
1 ripe vine tomato
1 carrot
5cm (2in) piece cucumber
5ml (1 tsp) ground flaxseed
2 stoned black or green olives (optional)
freshly ground black pepper
150ml (¼ pint) chilled filtered water

1 Put the sun-dried tomatoes and almonds in a small heatproof bowl and pour over the boiling water. Cover and leave to cool, then put in the fridge and soak for at least 1 hour, or overnight if preferred.

2   Tip the sun-dried tomatoes and almonds and remaining soaking liquid into a blender. Wash the fresh vine tomato and peel the carrot. Roughly chop the tomato, carrot and cucumber and add to the blender with the flaxseed and olives. Lightly season with ground black pepper and pour in the water.

3   Pulse the blender for a few seconds until the vegetables and almonds are finely chopped, then blend for about 45 seconds until smooth. Serve straight away.

COOK'S TIP

Olives add a slight saltiness and savoury flavour to this smoothie, but you can leave them out if you are on a low-salt diet.

PEAR, PLUM, RAISIN
AND WALNUT SMOOTHIE

Dried fruit, such as raisins and goji berries, are a concentrated source of energy and also act as a sweetener and thickener in smoothies. Pears and plums are both rich in pectin and soluble fibre, so are valuable in lowering harmful cholesterol levels in the body.

Serves 1

25g (1oz) raisins
25g (1oz) walnuts
15ml (1 tbsp) dried goji berries
200ml (7fl oz) filtered water
1 ripe pear
2 ripe plums

1 Put the raisins, walnuts and goji berries in a jug and pour over the water. Cover and leave to soak in the fridge for at least 1 hour, or overnight if preferred.
2 Wash the pear and plums. Cut the pear in quarters and remove the core, and halve the plums and remove the stones. Tip the soaked fruit, walnuts and water into a blender and add the pear and plums.
3 Pulse the blender for a few seconds until the fruit and walnuts are finely chopped, then blend for about 45 seconds until smooth.

4
BEAUTY ENHANCERS

PINK AND PEACHY

This smoothie uses canned coconut milk rather than coconut drinking milk. Coconut is great for your skin and can help to protect the body from harmful free-radicals that can accelerate ageing.

Serves 1

1 ripe peach or nectarine
50g (2oz) fresh or frozen raspberries
5ml (1 tsp) honey or agave syrup
5ml (1 tsp) acai berry powder (optional)
250ml (8fl oz) canned 'light' (reduced fat) coconut milk
ice, to serve

1   If using a peach, put it in a heatproof bowl and pour over just enough boiling water to cover. Leave for a minute, then remove and rinse under cold running water; peel off the skin and discard. If using a nectarine, wash well. Cut the peach or nectarine in half, remove the stone and roughly chop.

2   If using fresh raspberries, wash, then put in blender with the peach or nectarine. Add the acai berry powder if using and the coconut milk.

3   Pulse the blender until the fruit is finely chopped, then blend for about 30 seconds, until smooth. Pour into a glass with 3 or 4 ice cubes to chill the drink and serve straight away.

STRAWBERRY SUPER SKIN

Strawberries are rich in vitamin C, which is important for maintaining collagen levels to keep the skin smooth and supple. In addition, strawberries contain ellagic acid, which can destroy some of the toxins found in polluted air and cigarette smoke, both of which can damage your skin.

Serves 1

100g (4oz) fresh or frozen strawberries
100g (4oz) plain fromage frais
150ml (¼ pint) chilled semi-skimmed milk
15ml (1 tbsp) dried skimmed milk powder
5ml (1 tsp) lacuma powder (optional)

1   Wash the strawberries if using fresh, hull them, then cut any large ones in half. Put in a blender with the fromage frais, milk, skimmed milk powder and lacuma powder, if using.
2   Pulse the blender for a few seconds until the fruit is finely chopped, then blend for about 30 seconds until smooth. Serve straight away.

COOK'S TIP
Skimmed milk powder enriches the taste, thickens the texture and adds extra protein and calcium to this smoothie, but you can leave it out if you prefer.

PURPLE HEAVEN

This mixed fruit smoothie contains purple corn powder, which has a high antioxidant content and can boost collagen, as well as protecting against free-radical damage. If you prefer, acai berry powder can be used instead.

Serves 1

50g (2oz) fresh or frozen blueberries
50g (2oz) fresh or frozen blackberries
50g (2oz) fresh or frozen pitted black cherries
150ml (¼ pint) purple grape juice or filtered water, chilled
  if using fresh fruit
5ml (1 tsp) purple corn powder

1 Wash the fruit if using fresh, pat it dry on kitchen paper and put in a blender with the grape juice or water and purple corn powder.
2 Pulse the blender for a few seconds until the fruit is finely chopped, then blend for about 30 seconds until smooth.

COOK'S TIP
If you are using all frozen fruit, allow it to defrost at room temperature for about 10 minutes before blending.

PROTEIN PLUS

Protein is essential for repair and maintenance in the body and that includes the skin. This blend includes protein powder, which can be either soya or hemp, rather than the whey-based powders used by bodybuilders.

Serves 1

25g (1oz) blanched almonds
60ml (4 tbsp) boiling water
1 small ripe banana
200ml (7fl oz) chilled skimmed or semi-skimmed milk
15ml (1 tbsp) soya or hemp protein powder
2.5ml (½ tsp) pure vanilla extract (optional)
5ml (1 tsp) spirulina or powdered greens (optional)

1   Put the almonds in a heatproof bowl and pour over the boiling water. Cover and leave to cool. When the liquid is cold, put the bowl in the fridge and leave the nuts to soak for at least 30 minutes, or preferably for longer, up to 24 hours.

2   Peel the banana and slice or break it into smaller pieces. Put in a blender with the almonds and their soaking liquid, milk and protein powder, and the vanilla and spirulina or powdered greens, if using.

3   Pulse the blender for a few seconds until the almonds are finely chopped, then blend for about 30 seconds until smooth.

BLACKBERRY AND APPLE BLEND

Blackberries are one of the few fruits to contain vitamin E as well as vitamin C, a vital combination for protecting the skin against UV damage from sunlight, so enjoy this drink in the morning before you go out.

Serves 1

100g (4oz) fresh or frozen blackberries
1 eating apple
200ml (7fl oz) chilled coconut water
5ml (1 tsp) acai berry powder

1   Wash the blackberries if using fresh, and the apple. Quarter and core the apple and put in a blender with the blackberries. Pour over the coconut water and sprinkle over the acai berry powder, if using.

2   Pulse the blender for a few seconds until the blackberries and apple are finely chopped, then blend for about 30 seconds until fairly smooth.

COOK'S TIP
It is impossible to break down the blackberry pips completely, so your drink will still contain traces of these. If you really don't like the pips, blend the blackberries with 100ml (4fl oz) filtered water, then strain through a fine sieve to make a purée. Blend the blackberry purée with the apple, 100ml (4fl oz) chilled coconut water and acai berry powder, if using.

STRAWBERRY, SOYA AND SESAME SMOOTHIE

Tahini is made from sesame seeds, which are packed with zinc: an essential mineral for producing collagen and giving skin more elasticity. It gives this blend a subtle nutty flavour and thick and creamy texture.

Serves 1

75g (3oz) fresh or frozen strawberries
15ml (1 tbsp) tahini
60ml (4 tbsp) plain or strawberry soya yogurt
200ml (7fl oz) chilled sweetened soya milk or unsweetened
  soya milk and 5ml (1 tsp) maple syrup or honey

1   Wash the strawberries if using fresh, hull and halve any large ones. Put them in a blender with the tahini, yogurt and milk, adding the maple syrup or honey, if using.

2   Pulse the blender for a few seconds until the strawberries are finely chopped, then blend for about 30 seconds until smooth.

CUCUMBER AND SPINACH SMOOTHIE

Keeping well hydrated is good for your skin and this combination of greens provides many of the vital vitamins and minerals to help keep your complexion glowing. Lacuma powder adds a touch of sweetness and makes the spinach much more palatable.

Serves 1

small handful of baby spinach leaves, about 15g (½ oz)
½ small cucumber
175ml (6fl oz) chilled unsweetened apple juice or a mixture
   of apple juice and filtered water
10ml (2 tsp) lacuma powder

1   Wash the spinach and shake off excess water. Roughly chop the cucumber. Put in a blender with the apple juice and lacuma powder.

2   Pulse the blender for a few seconds until the spinach and cucumber are finely chopped, then blend for about 45 seconds until smooth.

CUCUMBER AND KALE CLEANSER

This smoothie contains ingredients that are known for their diuretic properties, so it can help to flush out toxins. It's also full of antioxidants, which can help to prevent free-radicals from causing cell degeneration.

Serves 1

¼ cucumber
½ stick celery
1 eating apple
small handful of kale leaves, about 15g (½oz)
5ml (1 tsp) lime juice
100ml (4fl oz) chilled filtered water

1 Wash the cucumber, celery, apple and kale and pat dry with kitchen paper or shake off excess water. Remove any large tough stems from the kale. Roughly chop the cucumber and celery and put in a blender. Quarter and core the apple and add to the blender with the kale, lime juice and water.
2 Pulse the blender for a few seconds until the fruit and vegetables are finely chopped, then blend for about 45 seconds until smooth.

GREEN FOR GO

The green colour of vegetables signifies chlorophyll, which has a cleansing action on your skin, so try to drink a green smoothie a couple of times a week. If you find smoothies made entirely of green vegetables a little unappetising, try adding sweet fruit, such as pineapple, to lighten the flavour.

Serves 1

small handful of kale, about 15g (½oz)
5cm (2in) piece cucumber
¼ small pineapple or half a 200g (7oz) can pineapple in
   natural juices
few sprigs of fresh parsley
75ml (3fl oz) chilled filtered water or juice from the canned
   pineapple
5ml (1 tsp) fresh or bottled lime juice
1.5ml (¼ tsp) spirulina powder
ice cubes, to serve

1   Wash the kale and shake off excess water, then remove any tough stems. Roughly chop the cucumber. If using fresh pineapple, remove the skin and central core if hard and roughly chop. If using canned pineapple, drain, reserving the juice.

2   Put the kale, cucumber, pineapple and parsley in a blender. Add the water or pineapple juice, lime juice and spirulina powder.

3   Pulse the blender for a few seconds until the pineapple and vegetables are finely chopped, then blend for about 45 seconds until smooth. Serve with a couple of ice cubes to chill the drink.

WATERCRESS AND YOGURT BLEND

This savoury smoothie contains a generous helping of low-fat yogurt, a great source of calcium that will help to keep your teeth strong and healthy. The high iron content of watercress can fight off fatigue, which often leads to cravings for high-sugar, unhealthy foods.

Serves 1

½ bunch watercress
250ml (8fl oz) low-fat bio yogurt
45ml (3 tbsp) skimmed milk
15ml (1 tbsp) pumpkin seeds
small pinch ground paprika

1 Wash the watercress under cold running water, then shake dry. Cut off the bottom half of the stalks and discard, then put the leaves and top half of the stalks into a blender with the yogurt, skimmed milk, pumpkin seeds and paprika.
2 Pulse the blender for a few seconds until the watercress and seeds are finely chopped, then blend for about 30 seconds until smooth.

PAPAYA AND BANANA SMOOTHIE

Papayas are an excellent age-defying food, as their high vitamin C content helps to maintain the skin's elasticity. Together with the vitamin E in wheat germ this smoothie is effective in protecting cells from damage and early wrinkling.

Serves 2

1 small ripe papaya
1 large ripe banana
60ml (4 tbsp) chilled filtered water
100ml (4fl oz) plain bio yogurt
15ml (1 tbsp) wheatgerm

1 Halve the papaya, scoop out the black seeds and discard. Thinly peel off the skin and cut the flesh into chunks. Peel the banana and slice or break into smaller pieces. Put the fruit in a blender with the water, yogurt and wheat germ.
2 Pulse the blender for a few seconds until the fruit is chopped, then blend for about 30 seconds until smooth.

MELON, RASPBERRY AND ELDERFLOWER BLEND

Elderflower cordial gives this blend a delicious and subtle floral flavour, perfect for sipping on a hot summer day. Melon has a high water content that makes this smoothie super-hydrating, keeping your skin plump and healthy.

Serves 1

¼ **honeydew melon**
50g (2oz) **fresh or frozen raspberries**
150ml (¼ pint) **chilled filtered water**
20ml (4 tsp) **elderflower cordial**
ice cubes, to serve

1   Scoop the seeds out of the melon and discard, then remove the skin and cut the flesh into chunks.
2   Put in a blender with the raspberries, water and elderflower cordial.
3   Pulse the blender for a few seconds until the melon and raspberries are finely chopped, then blend for about 30 seconds until smooth. Serve in a tall glass with ice.

WRINKLE SMOOTHER SMOOTHIE

While no food or drink can get rid of wrinkles, eating well can help to slow the inevitable ageing process; apples, cherries and barleygrass are all considered to be beneficial in keeping your skin in good condition and looking younger for longer.

Serves 1

1 eating apple
75g (3oz) fresh or frozen pitted dark cherries
150ml (¼ pint) chilled filtered water
5ml (1 tsp) barleygrass powder

1   Wash the apple and the cherries, if using fresh, before removing the stones. Quarter the apple, remove the core and roughly chop.
2   Put the fruit in a blender, pour over the chilled water, then sprinkle over the barleygrass powder.
3   Pulse the blender for a few seconds until the fruit is finely chopped, then blend for about 30 seconds until smooth.

PEACH BLUSH

Eating a very low-fat diet can play havoc with the condition of your hair and is no longer considered to be healthy. You should still avoid fatty junk food, but small amounts of higher-fat foods, such as coconut, can be good for you and will help to maintain a glossy mane.

Serves 1

25g (1oz) block creamed coconut
75ml (3fl oz) boiling water
1 ripe peach or nectarine
25g (1oz) fresh or frozen redcurrants
150ml (¼ pint) chilled skimmed milk
5ml (1 tsp) honey
2.5ml (½ tsp) orange flower water (optional)
ice cubes, to serve

1   Roughly chop the creamed coconut and put in a small heatproof bowl or jug. Pour over the boiling water and stir to dissolve. Leave to cool. Meanwhile, if using a peach, put in another heatproof bowl and pour over just enough boiling water to cover. Leave for a minute, then remove and rinse under cold running water; peel off the skin and discard. If using a nectarine, wash well. Cut the peach or nectarine in half, remove the stone and roughly chop the flesh.

2   Wash the redcurrants if using fresh and remove from the sprigs using the tines of a fork. Put in a blender with the peach or nectarine, then add the dissolved coconut, milk, honey and orange flower water if using.

3   Pulse the blender for a few seconds until the fruit is chopped, then blend for about 30 seconds until smooth. Serve with a couple of ice cubes to chill the drink.

CAPE GOOSEBERRY
AND BANANA SMOOTHIE

Cape gooseberries, also known as physalis, contain beta-carotene and vitamin C as well as potassium, which helps to counteract the effects that consumption of alcohol, coffee, sugar and salty foods can have on your body and your skin.

Serves 1

1 small ripe banana
100g (4oz) ripe cape gooseberries
5ml (1 tsp) honey or agave syrup
200ml (7fl oz) chilled rice milk

1   Peel the banana and slice or break into small pieces. Remove the paper husks from the cape gooseberries. Put the fruit in a blender, add the honey or agave syrup and pour over the milk.
2   Pulse the blender for a few seconds until the fruit is finely chopped, then blend for about 30 seconds until smooth.

GRAPEFRUIT, POMEGRANATE AND PEAR FLUSH

Bioflavonoids found in grapefruit help the body to absorb vitamin C, important for skin health. This drink provides all the daily vitamin C you need together with natural oestrogens found in pomegranate, which can help to prevent premature ageing.

Serves 1

1 ruby grapefruit
1 pomegranate
1 ripe pear
30ml (2 tbsp) cold filtered water
ice cubes, to serve

1 Peel the grapefruit using a small sharp knife, removing all the bitter white pith, then cut between the membranes to remove the segments, discarding any pips.

2 Cut the pomegranate in half, and using a citrus squeezer, extract as much juice as possible. Pour into the blender. Wash the pear, quarter and core, then add to the blender with the water.

3 Pulse the blender for a few seconds until the grapefruit and pear are finely chopped, then blend for about 30 seconds until smooth. Serve with a couple of ice cubes, to chill the drink.

ENGLISH ROSE

Stress can have a detrimental effect not only on your body, but also on your appearance. Your need for vitamin C increases when adrenaline levels are high, and strawberries contain an even higher amount than the equivalent weight of citrus fruit. This simple smoothie provides all your daily requirement of this vitamin.

Serves 1

150g (5oz) fresh or frozen strawberries
200ml (7fl oz) unsweetened rice milk, chilled if using fresh fruit
few drops of rose water

1   Wash the strawberries, if using fresh, then hull them and halve any large ones. Put in a blender with the rice milk and rose water.

2   Pulse the blender for a few seconds until the strawberries are finely chopped, then blend for about 30 seconds, until smooth.

COOK'S TIP
Rice milk has a subtly sweet flavour even when it contains no added sugar and is perfect for smoothies where the fruit would benefit from a little sweetener.

ALMOND AND ROSE MILK

Vitamin E, a fat-soluble vitamin, is considered to be nature's most effective antioxidant, protecting against free-radicals that can damage and age the skin. Almonds are a great source of the vitamin, but do need long soaking to blend smoothly.

Serves 1

75g (3oz) blanched almonds
2 stoned dates, such as Medjool (optional)
250ml (8fl oz) chilled filtered water, plus extra for soaking
few drops of rose water

1 Put the almonds in a bowl and pour in enough filtered water to cover them by about 5cm (2in). Cover with cling film and leave to soak at room temperature for 6 hours, or for up to 24 hours in the fridge.

2 Drain the almonds, discarding the soaking water. Put in a blender with the dates, if using, then pour in the chilled water and add a few drops of rose water.

3 Pulse the blender for a few seconds until the nuts and dates are finely chopped, then blend for about 45 seconds until smooth.

COOK'S TIP
Dates will make the milk a dark, creamy colour and both sweeten and thicken the drink, but you can leave them out if you prefer.

STRAWBERRY AND WATERMELON REFRESHER

Watermelon has a high water content – hence its name. But it's not just useful for hydrating the skin; the fruit also contains a number of beneficial vitamins and minerals. The seeds are rich in zinc and selenium, so only remove the very large tough ones; smaller ones will blend into the juice, giving it a speckled effect.

Serves 1

1 large wedge of watermelon or half a 'baby' watermelon, about 250g (9oz) flesh in total
50g (2oz) fresh or frozen strawberries
2.5ml (½ tsp) balsamic vinegar
5ml (1 tsp) honey
ice, to serve

1 Cut the watermelon flesh into chunks, discarding any large hard pips. Wash and hull the strawberries if using fresh. Put the watermelon and strawberries in a blender and add the balsamic vinegar and honey.
2 Pulse the blender for a few seconds until the watermelon and strawberries are finely chopped, then blend for about 30 seconds, until smooth. Pour into a glass and add an ice cube to chill the drink; more if you used fresh rather than frozen strawberries.

WATERMELON AND GINGER SHARBAT

Watermelon consists of over 90 per cent water and can be blended into a smoothie without any additional liquid, so here it is simply flavoured with a little ginger to add a spicy kick. It contains vitamin C and beta-carotene plus the antioxidant lycopene, which helps neutralise free-radicals.

Serves 1

1 large wedge of watermelon or half a 'baby' watermelon, about 250g (9oz) flesh in total
5ml (1 tsp) freshly grated ginger (see page 3)
ice cubes, to serve

1 Cut the watermelon flesh into chunks, discarding any large hard pips, and put it in a blender with the ginger.
2 Pulse the blender for a few seconds until the watermelon is finely chopped, then blend for about 30 seconds until smooth. Serve with ice, to chill the drink.

SKIN PLUMPER

Cucumbers are rich in potassium, which helps skin to retain its elasticity and maintains the water balance within cells. Here it is combined with mild-tasting lettuce, a handful of blueberries and some ground flaxseed for a delicious green blend.

Serves 1

¼ cucumber
25g (1oz) soft lettuce leaves
50g (2oz) fresh or frozen blueberries
5ml (1 tsp) ground flaxseed
200ml (7fl oz) unsweetened apple juice or a mixture of juice and filtered water, chilled if using fresh blueberries

1 Wash the cucumber, lettuce leaves and blueberries if using fresh. Shake excess water from the lettuce leaves and roughly chop with the cucumber. Put in a blender with the blueberries, flaxseed and apple juice.
2 Pulse the blender for a few seconds until the vegetables and blueberries are finely chopped, then blend for about 30 seconds until smooth.

MELON AND KALE SMOOTHIE

Fruits and vegetables with yellow, orange or dark green pigments contain carotenoids, which are converted to vitamin A, vital for the health of your skin and eyes. Here, sweet and juicy cantaloupe melon is combined with kale to make a surprisingly tasty blend.

Serves 1

¼ ripe cantaloupe melon
small handful of kale, about 15g (½oz)
60ml (4 tbsp) filtered water
ice, to serve

1 Cut the rind off the melon and discard the pips. Roughly chop and put in a blender. Wash the kale and shake off excess water, discarding any tough stalks. Add to the blender with the water.
2 Pulse the blender for a few seconds until the melon and kale are finely chopped, then blend for about 45 seconds until smooth. Serve with a few ice cubes to chill the drink.

FRESH FRUIT AND GREENS

Chlorella encourages cellular renewal and repair, so as well as being highly nutritious, it is a great beauty aid. It does have a strong flavour, so use in small quantities along with your favourite fresh fruit. When you get accustomed to the taste, you can add a little more to the blend.

Serves 1

1 small ripe ripe banana
100g (4oz) fresh berries, such as strawberries, raspberries, pitted cherries or chopped fresh peaches
100ml (4fl oz) chilled unsweetened fruit juice or skimmed or semi-skimmed milk
5ml (1 tsp) chlorella powder
ice, to serve

1　Peel the banana and slice or break into pieces and put in a blender. Wash the berries if necessary and add to the blender with the fruit juice or milk and chlorella powder.
2　Pulse the blender for a few seconds until the fruit is finely chopped, then blend for about 20 seconds until smooth. Pour into a glass and add a few ice cubes to chill.

TOMATO, AVOCADO AND CHILLI BLITZ

This delicious rejuvenating combination of fresh tomatoes and creamy avocado is spiced with fresh chilli. Tomatoes are rich in the antioxidant lycopene, which can repair skin damage and help to protect from sunburn.

Serves 1

4 vine-ripened tomatoes
½ medium-hot red chilli
½ ripe avocado
75ml (3fl oz) chilled filtered water
freshly ground black pepper (optional)

1   Put the tomatoes in a heatproof bowl and pour over just enough boiling water to cover them. Leave for 1 minute, then drain and rinse the tomatoes under cold running water. Peel off the skins (they should slip off easily), then quarter the tomatoes and remove the seeds. Put the tomatoes in a blender.

2   Remove the seeds from the chilli (unless you like your smoothie really hot and spicy) and add the chilli flesh to the blender. Remove the skin and stone from the avocado, roughly chop the flesh and add to the blender with the water and a little freshly ground black pepper, if liked.

3   Pulse the blender for a few seconds until the tomatoes, chilli and avocado are finely chopped, then blend for about 30 seconds until smooth. Check the consistency and if you prefer it a little thinner add a few more spoonfuls of water and briefly blend again.

APPLE AND BLACKCURRANT BLEND

Stress, hormonal changes and the ageing process can all lead to increased hair loss, resulting in thinner and less healthy-looking hair. Counteract this by ensuring you have enough zinc in your daily diet; this drink contains plenty.

Serves 1

1 eating apple
50g (2oz) fresh or frozen blackcurrants
15ml (1 tbsp) sunflower seeds
5ml (1 tsp) lacuma powder, honey, maple syrup or agave syrup
5ml (1 tsp) acai berry powder
100ml (4fl oz) filtered water, chilled if using fresh fruit

1   Wash the apple, quarter and core. Wash the blackcurrants if fresh and remove the berries from the sprigs with the tines of a fork. Put the apple and blackcurrants in a blender with the sunflower seeds, lacuma powder, honey, maple syrup or agave syrup, acai berry powder and water.
2   Pulse the blender for a few seconds until the fruit and seeds are finely chopped, then blend for about 45 seconds until fairly smooth.

COOK'S TIP
If time allows, soak the sunflower seeds in the water in a covered bowl in the fridge for an hour or two, or overnight if you prefer; you will get a smoother, thicker blend.

BLACKBERRY AND BEETROOT BLEND

Blackberries are full of vitamin C, which is needed for the formation of collagen, a structural protein that helps keep the skin elastic and anchors teeth into the gums. It is particularly important for regular drinkers and smokers, who may be at risk of deficiency of the vitamin.

Serves 1

75g (3oz) fresh or frozen blackberries
1 small beetroot, about 100g (4oz)
200ml (7fl oz) cranberry juice, or a mixture of juice and
  filtered water, chilled if using fresh blackberries

1 Rinse the blackberries if using fresh and put in a blender. Top and tail the beetroot and peel thinly. Roughly chop and add to the blender with the cranberry juice.
2 Pulse the blender for a few seconds until the beetroot is finely chopped, then blend for about 45 seconds until fairly smooth (the drink will still have a few flecks of beetroot in it).

MANGO LASSI

This fruity blend originates in India and makes a refreshing drink in hot weather. Mangoes are rich in cell-protecting vitamins and phytochemicals and make thick and creamy smoothies.

Serves 1

½ ripe mango
75ml (3fl oz) chilled filtered water
10ml (2 tsp) lime juice
5ml (1 tsp) honey or agave syrup
150ml (¼ pint) plain bio yogurt
crushed ice or ice cubes, to serve

1   Using a small, sharp knife, peel the mango, then slice the flesh away from the stone. Roughly chop and place in a blender with the water, lime juice and honey or agave syrup.
2   Pulse the blender for a few seconds until the mango is finely chopped, then blend for about 15 seconds until fairly smooth. Add the yogurt and blend again for about 15 seconds until smooth.
3   Half-fill a tall glass with crushed ice or ice cubes and pour over the mango lassi. Leave for a minute or two for the drink to chill.

COOK'S TIP
Lassi is usually a very sweet drink. To avoid needing to add more sweetener than suggested in the recipe, use a very ripe, sweet mango.

TROPICAL FRUIT AND FLAX

Flaxseed has a huge number of health benefits and contains at least 75 times the amount of lignans than other plant foods, making it a great source of antioxidants. Ground flaxseed adds a slightly nutty flavour to both sweet and savoury smoothies.

Serves 1

½ fresh ripe mango
1 small ripe banana
small handful of baby spinach leaves, about 15g (½oz)
about 150ml (¼ pint) chilled pineapple juice
10ml (2 tsp) ground flaxseed

1   Using a small, sharp knife, peel the mango, then slice the flesh away from the stone. Roughly chop and place in a blender. Peel the banana and slice or break it into smaller pieces. Wash the spinach and shake off excess water. Add the banana, spinach, pineapple juice and flaxseed to the blender.
2   Pulse the blender for a few seconds, then blend for about 30 seconds until smooth. Check the consistency and if you prefer it a little thinner, add a few more spoonfuls of pineapple juice or filtered water and blend again.

MELON AND PEAR SHINER

Enjoy radiant skin with this cleansing blend of honeydew melon, pear and red grapes. It's a great drink to enjoy at any time of the day and needs absolutely no sweetening.

Serves 1

½ small ripe honeydew melon
1 ripe pear
75g (3oz) seedless red grapes
2.5ml (½ tsp) grated fresh ginger (see page 3), optional

1   Using a sharp knife, cut the melon into quarters, scoop out the seeds and slice the flesh away from the skin. Wash the pear and grapes, then cut the pear into quarters and remove the core. Put the melon, pear and grapes into a blender and add the ginger, if using.

2   Pulse the blender for a few seconds until the fruit is finely chopped, then blend for about 30 seconds until smooth. If the blend is a little thick, add a few spoonfuls of filtered water and briefly blend again.

GOLDEN GREAT

This is a delicious, sweet and slightly tangy blend and contains ground turmeric – a vibrant yellow spice that adds an earthy flavour and helps the body to release toxins.

Serves 2

1 ripe mango
½ large ripe cantaloupe melon
2.5ml (½ tsp) ground turmeric
5ml (1 tsp) fresh or bottled lime or lemon juice
45ml (3 tbsp) filtered water
ice, to serve

1   Using a sharp knife, cut the mango lengthwise on either side of the stone. Peel thinly, then slice the flesh away from the stone.

2   Cut the melon into quarters, scoop out the seeds and slice the flesh away from the skin. Roughly chop, then put the mango and melon in a blender. Add the turmeric, lime or lemon juice and water.

3   Pulse the blender for a few seconds until finely chopped, then blend for about 30 seconds until smooth. Divide between two glasses, adding a couple of ice cubes to each to chill the drink.

ANTI-AGER

This smoothie is full of anti-ageing ingredients, including hempseed oil, which contains amino acids and essential fatty acids that play a vital role in maintaining young-looking skin.

Serves 1

75g (3oz) **fresh or frozen blueberries**
75g (3oz) **silken tofu**
150ml (¼ pint) **chilled coconut drinking milk**
10ml (2 tsp) **hempseed oil**

1 Rinse the blueberries if using fresh and put them in a blender with the tofu, coconut drinking milk and hempseed oil.
2 Pulse the blender for a few seconds until the blueberries are finely chopped, then blend for about 20 seconds until smooth.

GOJI BERRY AND CRANBERRY BLITZ

Also known as wolfberries, goji berries grow in the Himalayas. As they are too fragile to be transported whole, they are sold as powder, juice or dried berries. The latter are a stunning deep orangey-red colour and benefit from pre-soaking before being made into smoothies.

Serves 1

30ml (2 tbsp) dried goji berries
30ml (2 tbsp) dried sweetened cranberries
250ml (8fl oz) coconut water

1 Put the dried goji berries and cranberries in a jug and pour over the coconut water. Cover with cling film and leave to soak and chill in the fridge for at least 4 hours, or overnight if you prefer.
2 Pour the mixture into a blender, pulse for a few seconds until the berries are finely chopped, then blend for about 30 seconds until fairly smooth.

GOJI BERRY AND COCONUT SMOOTHIE

Goji berries are packed with amino acids, trace minerals and a huge amount of vitamin C. Here they are blended with creamy coconut milk to make a peachy-pink smoothie that is good news for your hair.

Serves 1

30ml (2 tbsp) dried goji berries
60ml (4 tbsp) filtered water
250ml (8fl oz) chilled coconut drinking milk
5ml (1 tsp) lacuma powder (optional)

1 Put the goji berries and water in a small bowl, cover with cling film and leave to soak and chill in the fridge for at least 4 hours, or overnight if you prefer.
2 Tip the soaked berries and liquid into a blender and add the coconut drinking milk and the lacuma powder, if using.
3 Pulse the blender for a few seconds until the goji berries are finely chopped, then blend for about 30 seconds, until smooth.

CHOCOLATE AND CASHEW NUT SMOOTHIE

Cacao is rich in iron, promoting healthy glowing skin. Here, it is blended with soaked nuts to make a chocolate-flavoured nut milk. Cashews have a mild, slightly sweet flavour, so no additional sweetening should be necessary.

Serves 1

75g (3oz) cashew nuts
250ml (8fl oz) chilled filtered water, plus extra for soaking
15ml (1 tbsp) cacao powder
few drops of pure vanilla extract

1 Put the nuts in a bowl and pour over enough filtered water to cover them by 5cm (2in). Cover the bowl with cling film and leave to soak for 2–3 hours, or longer in the fridge if you prefer.
2 Drain the nuts and put in a blender with the chilled water, cacao powder and vanilla extract.
3 Pulse the blender for a few seconds until the nuts are finely chopped, then blend for about 30 seconds until smooth.

INDEX